A GREEN GUIDE TO TRADITIONAL
COUNTRY FOODS

A GREEN GUIDE TO TRADITIONAL
COUNTRY FOODS

Discover traditional ways to cure and smoke,
pickle and preserve, make cheese, bake, and more

GENERAL EDITOR HENRIETTA GREEN

Additional text by Jenny Linford

CICO BOOKS
LONDON NEW YORK
www.cicobooks.com

Published in 2011 by CICO Books
An imprint of Ryland Peters & Small Ltd
519 Broadway, 5th Floor
New York NY 10012

10 9 8 7 6 5 4 3 2 1

www.cicobooks.com

Copy editors: Alison Bolus, Kay Halsey, and Eleanor van Zandt
Designer: Louise Leffler
For additional credits see page 192

ISBN: 978 1 907563 28 7

Printed in China

Contents

Introduction

I have always believed that food, essential for our survival, is a mirror of our society. Why and how we prepared what we prepared to eat all those centuries ago provide fascinating insights into our social history. Look at the produce and you get a sense of how our lands were farmed, the types of livestock raised, and the importance placed on certain foodstuffs.

Back then, the struggle for survival was paramount; think of when there was no electricity, no refrigerators or freezers, no cans, the most basic of farm machinery, and no means of over-wintering the livestock and you realize how our forefathers must have struggled. Most of the traditional country foods were based on preserving—by salting, curing, smoking, baking, pickling, or drying—the seasonal gluts for the long cold dark days ahead.

Modern technology has allowed us to master preservation but although the motives may have changed, the crafts remain. Undoubtedly they have been adapted—salt, for example, is no longer used in such large quantities, with the resulting tastes more fitting for our subtle appetites—but the principles are still the same.

This book is a celebration of these food crafts, then and now, and the craftsmen and women who continue to practice them.

As I travel about the countryside meeting them, I never fail to be struck by their passion and dedication. Whether they are newcomers who have made the deliberate decision to move away from life in the city or families who have handed down their secrets from father to son over the generations, they all share a bond, a common interest, and goal. It is a worthy one—the ambition to make "The Best."

Their life may still be tough but, by and large, they enjoy it. Most work extremely hard and their reward, believe it or not, comes from the satisfaction in producing good food, a "job well done," and the pleasure of their customers' enjoyment. As we chat away, they reveal insights and an attention to details that are awe-inspiring and I never cease to wonder at their enthusiasm and generosity.

Glance through these pages and you will see how these men and women are happy to share their "secrets," the techniques

Left: Cider vinegar maturing in an open jar covered with muslin
Right: The all-important kneading process
Far right: Butter being shaped before packaging

that transforms the ordinary into the extra-ordinary. Read our highlighted producer profiles and you will see what I mean. They talk about fussing over a product as if it were their child; recognizing when it is ready by how it might feel in the hand, look in the pan, or smell in the air. These are instinctive reactions that come through practice and awareness. To the craftsmen, it is second nature, to us these are skills to which we must aspire.

So when you start trying the recipes—making your very first soft cheese, for example—may I encourage you to not only buy the best ingredients (a good milk will transform the flavor) but to keep the faith. I remember my first cheeses, made in my larder years ago. Lumpy and exceptionally gritty, if only I had known then about handling the curds! But it is only by practicing that you, too, will learn and hone your instincts.

of their craft, which means we can not only better understand their produce and appreciate its values, but also set about making it for ourselves. And if you're lucky enough to spend time with them discussing the merits (or de-merits) of one product against another, you soon come to realize just how many details, layers, and stages can exist in creating, say, nothing more complex than a loaf of bread.

When I was just starting out in the world of food, I remember meeting a wise and particularly seasoned (forgive the pun) producer whose family had been curing award-winning hams to critical acclaim. Not only did he invite me into his curing room and spend hours explaining the distinctions between the seemingly random ingredients, but he also told me of his guiding principle. "Quality," he explained, "is like a chain. And every link—from the breed of pig, how it is fed, reared, slaughtered, and hung, to the ingredients of the cure, how long it is cured for, and even how often it is turned in the cure—has to be strongly forged. Each one matters. Each one affects the eating quality. And it's true for any and every product you are attempting to produce."

The links I have since added to my quality chain are passion and instinct. These are characteristics successful producers have in abundance but are difficult to pin down—a pity, as so often it is that very commitment and "just knowing"

If you need final encouragement, remember a recipe is no more than a set of instructions that tells you how to make or prepare something with virtually no allowances for techniques. This was struck home forcibly when I went to a cook-in. A group of about ten of us—all food or cookery writers—was given aprons, the same recipe for cheese soufflé, and told to get started. Some beat egg whites forcibly, others more languidly; some worked meticulously and others were far more slapdash. As for the soufflés, if some puffed up perfectly, others sank in despair. Each one was different in taste, texture, and appearance.

Your techniques are bound to vary from one day to the next as well as from any other cook. So if your fudge is not as smooth as silk the first time around—give it another whirl. Don't be put off. Think of the generations of craftsman who have gone before you. And above all else—enjoy.

Henrietta Green

Left: Light and fluffy marshmallows, delicious when dipped in melted chocolate
Right: Lemon and ginger syrup, a comforting and soothing drink that is perfect when you have a cold

Chapter I

THE DAIRY

Since ancient times, dairy products have been an important source of food. Milk—which is where all dairy products start—is a remarkably versatile foodstuff, which can be both drunk in liquid form and used to make a large range of semi-solid and solid foodstuffs. For thousands of years, humans have domesticated grass-grazing ruminants such as cows, goats, and sheep in order to use their protein-rich milk in many different forms. Although sheep and goats were used as dairy animals centuries before cattle, in the West it is the cow, peacefully grazing on lush, green grass in a field, that is the iconic image of a dairy animal.

For centuries, dairy animals were laboriously milked by hand —a process that is nowadays largely mechanized. In the period before refrigeration, however, valuable, labor-intensive milk was highly perishable, and so people had to devise ingenious ways to transform it into other foods, exploiting its fatty content to create a number of different dairy products, such as cheese, cream, butter, and yogurt. Making *cheese* from milk was historically a way of transforming nutritious milk into a food that was delicious in its own right and could also be stored and eaten safely for longer than milk itself. Long enjoyed as a luxury, *cream* is the fat-rich part of milk, which rises naturally to the surface in milk that hasn't been homogenized (that is, treated to disperse the fat evenly throughout the milk). Cream, in its turn, is turned into *butter* through the process of churning, which removes most of the cream's water content to leave behind the butterfat, which is valued for its flavor, texture, and enhanced keeping qualities.

Finally, yogurt, which is created naturally when milk ferments, thickening into a semi-solid foodstuff with a distinctive sour tang, has a very long history as a dairy product.

The dairy—a cool, often tiled room—was traditionally a predominantly female workplace. It was here that the farmer's wife or the dairymaid turned the milk (freshly milked by her early that morning) into dairy products such as butter, cream, cheese, and yogurt. With industrialization and mechanization, however, we have largely lost touch with the centuries-old processes by which milk was used to make other foods, though our rich dairy tradition still offers a source of inspiration for the home cook. Making your own soft cheese is both simple and satisfying, and taking cream and transforming it into butter, either by using a food processor or simply by shaking it for several minutes in a jar, is a wonderful piece of kitchen alchemy that is great fun for children to try.

Cheese

It is thought that the discovery that liquid milk could be transformed into solid cheese dates back thousands of years to when early shepherds found that the milk they had stored in animal stomach or hide containers had naturally curdled and formed a soft curdlike cheese. Many artisanal cheese makers prefer using "raw" or unpasteurized milk either from their own dairy animals or from a source that they know and trust, feeling that this produces a more flavorful and interesting cheese, which reflects the origin of the milk from which it is made.

Of all the dairy foods, cheese is the most varied. It is made by curdling milk by adding acidulating agents such as lemon juice or rennet, the latter containing the enzyme rennin (also known as chymosin), which occurs naturally in the stomachs of mammals. The cheese maker then works with the curds to produce the cheese required. Many intricate factors, such as the temperature the milk and curds are heated to and for how long, the bacterial cultures added to the milk to start the curdling process, and how the moisture is extracted from the curds go toward creating cheese, which makes cheese making a fascinating process. There are literally hundreds of different cheeses made, ranging in size, texture, and flavor from small, fresh, delicate soft cheeses – eaten when only a few days old – to huge, hard cheeses, such as cloth-bound, traditional Somerset Cheddar, firm-textured and with a long-lasting savory finish, or blue-veined cheeses such as Roquefort, with their characteristic salty-sweet tang. It is extraordinary to think that such diversity all starts with one ingredient: milk.

Professional cheese makers nowadays use what are called starter cultures, made from a mixture of rennet and lactic acid bacteria. The curdling process creates both soft curds (made from coagulated proteins called caseins) and whey (the remaining liquid part of the milk). The whey is drained from the curds, and these curds are then worked on in different

Opposite left: The all-important maturing process to give Cheddar its distinct flavor
Opposite right: Butter being pressed by hand to remove any water
Right: Dorstone (Herefordshire) goat cheese rolled in ash

Above: Perroche cheese from Neal's Yard Creamery

ways to create different cheeses. A young, delicate-textured goat cheese, for example, can be created by carefully ladling the curds into small molds and allowing the curds to drain under their own weight. Cheeses with a firmer texture are made by pressing the curds in molds, meshing them together. A way of shaping cheese that is very characteristic of British cheese making is the wrapping of muslin around a large, molded cheese before setting it aside to ripen for many months. This technique is used to hold the cheese together, allowing it to develop texture and flavor, and is traditionally used for making cheeses such as farmhouse Cheddar.

One of the striking features of the cheese-making process is the way cheese makers work with bacteria to create the cheeses they want, using the bacteria to affect the flavor, texture, and aroma. Creating the right conditions in which to encourage the required bacteria to thrive and grow is part of the craft of cheese making. Different bacterial cultures are added to the milk at the beginning of the cheese-making process to create specific flavors and types of cheeses. In traditional Swiss cheese making, for example, a bacterium called *Propionibacteria shermanii*, also known as the "hole-maker," creates carbon dioxide bubbles inside the cheese, which result in the holes characteristic of Swiss cheeses such as Emmental.

Blue cheeses, such as Stilton or Roquefort, are made by adding a bacterial culture called *Penicillium roqueforti* as a starter. In order to allow these bacteria to grow and thrive, blue cheeses are traditionally never pressed, with the curd instead piled loosely into molds. The bacteria turn blue-green in reaction to the air, so to ensure the distinctive blue veining, the cheeses are pierced with long rods to let the air enter the cheese, allowing blueing to take place within the paste.

Several types of cheeses may be brined in a salt solution while still very young (within 24 hours of making). Later on, another technique, washed rind, can come into play. This is done by wiping or soaking or washing the outside of the cheese with a bacteria, a salt solution, or even an alcohol-based solution. As the natural bacteria grows, it creates a coating or skin on the cheese—think of the sticky orange-red outside of France's Epoisses, Ireland's Gubbeen or England's Stinking Bishop.

Meet the producer: Cothi Valley Goats

"My real passion is the goats," admits Lynne Beard of Cothi Valley Goats, in Wales, who, together with her husband, Richard, keeps 350 goats (a mixture of white-coated British Saanens and brown-coated British Toggenburgs) on her farm. "They're so individual; no two goats are the same. They have a wicked sense of humor and can drive you round the bend, but they're beautiful.

"Contented animals make for better produce," observes Lynne, who makes sures that her beloved goats lead as natural a life as possible. "They forage outside from spring to autumn, though if it's wet, no goat will put its hoof outside the barn! They have access to a large yard all year round. We don't use any artificial daylight to trick them into producing milk; instead, we have half the herd kid one year, the other half kid the next. That way I always have some goat milk to work with."

The unpasteurized milk from their herd is turned by Lynne into seven different cheeses, ranging from Luddesdown, a soft, fresh cheese with a "delicate, lemony, lactic" flavor, sold when just a few days old, to Tally Las, a month-old blue cheese, with a creamy texture and "delicate" blue flavor.

"There's something very satisfying about making cheese using milk from your own animals; we don't use any bought-in milk. I know my animals are healthy and that the milk is safe. I prefer using unpasteurized milk, as I feel it gives the cheeses a better flavor, more individuality and character. Everyone goes on about spring milk (milk from goats calved in the spring), but I love autumn milk. There's less of it, but it has a great fat and protein content that makes wonderful, velvety, creamy cheese. I can feel the difference in the curd in autumn. Goat's milk curd is very delicate, so you have to treat it gently. You can't bash it about and you mustn't stir it too hard."

The Beards then sell their cheeses direct at farmers' markets and food festivals. "That's the good bit, when, after all the hard work—and it is hard work—people come up and tell you how much they've enjoyed your cheese and you know what you're doing is appreciated."

Cream and butter

Historically considered to be treats rather than everyday ingredients, cream and butter are both by-products of the natural butterfat in milk. Traditionally, cream was created by simply setting fresh milk to one side and allowing the cream to rise naturally to the surface of the milk, then skimming it off. Creating cream in this way, however, is on the whole no longer possible, because most, by far, of the milk that is sold commercially has been homogenized—that is, treated in order to disperse the fat evenly within the milk. This process makes milk taste creamier and look whiter, because the cream-colored particles are scattered throughout the milk. Alongside homogenization, the milk is usually pasteurized, which means that it is heat-treated to kill off any bacteria within the milk. As a result, nowadays cream is produced using centrifugal force to separate the cream from the milk.

Above: Shaping butter the traditonal way using butter hands

Butter is made from cream, which is worked until the butterfat present in the cream separates from the buttermilk. Both Britain and the United States favor what is termed "sweet butter," which means that it is made with fresh cream. (The term is sometimes misapplied to unsalted butter.) In continental Europe, they favor "cultured cream butter," in which the cream is mixed with particular lactic acid bacteria and allowed to "ripen" (i.e. sour very slightly) before being turned into butter; the result is butter that is subtly more flavorful than sweet butter. While most butter is made from cow's milk, it can also be made from the milk of other dairy animals, such as goats, sheep, or water buffalo. Although butter does have keeping qualities because of its high fat content, these can be extended considerably by clarifying it—that is, by melting and simmering it very gently to cook off all the water, then straining off and discarding the milk solids. The resulting golden liquid is clarified butter (known as ghee in India), which is valued by cooks for its rich, buttery flavor and the fact that it has a higher smoking point than ordinary butter when used as a cooking fat.

Buttermilk

As its name suggests, buttermilk was traditionally a by-product of the butter-making process: the white milky liquid created when cream is turned into butter. Nowadays, most

Meet the Producer: Ivy House Dairy Farm

A herd of 230 golden-coated Jersey cattle are at the heart of Ivy House Dairy Farm, in Somerset, Geoff and Kim Bowles' organic farm. Jersey cattle are noted for the high butterfat content of their milk, which gives it a characteristic deep yellow color and full creamy flavor. The Bowles sell the milk from their herd simply as milk (from skim and 1% fat to whole milk) and also use it to make their own cream, clotted cream (a kind of extra-thick cream produced by heating), and buttermilk. Although the Bowles do pasteurize their milk, they don't homogenize it, as is standard these days, so the cream rises to the top of the milk to form a layer on the surface.

The son of a dairy farmer himself, Geoff Bowles "fell in love" with Jersey cattle and decided to set up a farm with a Jersey herd. "To my mind, they're the only pure dairy breed," explains Geoff. "The calves are like deer; there's no meat on them. Dairy is what they're for." The golden color of the milk from the high butterfat content "comes as a surprise to people now" because they're used to the pale milk that comes from

Friesians, a dual-purpose breed used for milk and for beef. "Jersey cattle are lovely to work with," declares Geoff. "The cows have the nicest temperament, though the bulls have very bad tempers so you have to be careful."

The butter making came about one January when, due to lower demand for cream in the winter, they found themselves with an excess of cream and decided to use it make their own butter by hand in the traditional way. This small-scale production is carried out by hand, a much gentler process than mechanized butter making. "Whereas mass-manufactured butter is created through the use of sheer force, with the butter extruded from the machine, ours is worked by hand to force out the moisture, patted out by hand, wrapped by hand," explains Geoff. "The biggest demand for our butter comes from catering; pastry chefs love working with it. Not only does it have a lot of flavor, because we make it by hand, it seems to have a great elasticity to it that mass-produced butter lacks."

commercially sold buttermilk is made by adding a fermenting culture to milk, in the same way as for making yogurt, then breaking down the resulting set curds to create a thick, smooth liquid with a sour tang. Buttermilk is prized in baking because it adds flavor and tenderness to baked goods such as biscuits and soda bread and pancakes.

Hygienic conditions are vital when making your own buttermilk, so sterilize the cheesecloth used to strain the curd by boiling it for ten minutes before use, and pour boiling water over the utensils you will use.

Right: Cream being prepared at Ivy House Dairy for sale at the farmer's market

Yogurt

The natural presence of lactic acid bacteria in milk is key to a number of fermented milk products that are created by encouraging these microbes to multiply. As they grow, they release lactic acid into the milk, creating a sour flavor that is characteristic of fermented milk products. Yogurt, the most widely known of these products, was made for thousands of years in many parts of the world, including Central Asia and India, but was not introduced to the United States and Western Europe until the early part of the twentieth century. Other fermented milk products include soured cream, crème fraîche, and buttermilk. Originally, these processes occurred naturally through the presence of bacteria in the milk, but nowadays commercial producers create them in carefully controlled conditions by adding particular strains of bacteria.

Yogurt is made by first heating the milk, then cooling it, in order to allow a fermentation process to begin—a process triggered by adding the bacteria, usually in the form of "live" yogurt. (The description "live" yogurt refers to the fact that it has been made with a live bacterial culture and still contains these benign bacteria. The belief that certain bacteria found in yogurt aid digestion is leading to manufacturers' adding "probiotic" bacteria—that is, bacteria that are beneficial to health—to yogurt.) The milk is then put somewhere to incubate at the correct temperature to allow the bacteria to thrive and turn the milk into set yogurt. A general rule of thumb is that the longer the yogurt sets, the firmer and more acid it becomes. Straining yogurt through fine muslin to remove the whey is a traditional way to thicken its texture, with yogurts such as Greek yogurt being an example of this. The longer the yogurt is strained, the thicker it is, becoming, in effect, a soft cheese, such as the Middle Eastern labne, which is made made by straining yogurt for several hours.

Left: Yogurt is a popular healthy option for breakfast or dessert due to the healthy bacteria present in it

Meet the producer: Neal's Yard Creamery

Working with his small Herefordshire dairy, Charlie Westhead carefully makes a small range of subtly flavorful dairy products using both goat's milk, from which he makes three cheeses, and cow's milk, from which he makes one cheese, yogurt, and crème fraîche.

"I'm making different styles of small cheeses," he explains; "the sorts of cheeses a farmer in France with some goats might make." The start of his working day sees Charlie collecting the milk he uses from two local farms, who have supplied him with "lovely milk" for many years, arriving back home with the milk "in time for breakfast." For his cheeses, Charlie uses a traditional kid rennet from France, which he finds "gives the best flavor" and produces "nice, silky" curds.

The first cheese that Charlie made commercially was Perroche, a French-inspired fresh goat cheese, which he continues to produce to this day. Making Perroche requires "very gentle handling," as goat's milk makes very fragile curds. The milk is left to coagulate overnight, then the curd is cut into cubes with a steel ruler in the bucket and carefully transferred into plastic molds. "It's very delicate curd, so if I drop a cube just six inches onto the surface, it breaks." The curd is left to self-drain in the mold for an hour, then filled up again and left to drain overnight. The following day the cheeses are brined in a brine solution for 12 minutes. "This firms up the cheese," explains Charlie, "and adds salt for flavor and for keeping." The dainty cheeses are then sold either just plain or coated with rosemary, tarragon, or dill.

In addition to his cheeses, Charlie's company, Neal's Yard Creamery, is noted for its yogurt and crème fraîche. "To make these I need to create a receptive growing medium for the cultures that I add," explains Charlie. First, the milks are enriched with a little cream (for the yogurt) and pure double (heavy) cream (for the crème fraîche) and are heated to pasteurization point to eliminate other bacteria. The yogurt milk is then cooled to 113°F and the crème fraîche to 77°F, temperatures at which the cultures will thrive. While still liquid, the warm milk and cream are poured into pots and incubated until they thicken and set, the yogurt for 3 to 4 hours and the crème fraîche for 16 hours at a cooler temperature. Both the quality of the locally sourced milk and the starter cultures he uses "add a depth of flavor" to both his yogurt and his crème fraîche, which, in his words, have "a long, rich flavor and longer rounder finish, not just a simple acidic kick."

Sourcing the ingredients

Anybody who makes dairy products will tell you that using good-quality milk is essential to the process. Some artisanal cheese makers choose to work with unpasteurized, or "raw," milk, rather than pasteurized milk, valuing the flavor it creates. Raw milk for domestic use is very hard to track down but can be found at farm shops in some states.

The vast majority of commercially available milks have been pasteurized and also generally homogenized (see page 12). Pasteurized milk and cream can be used for making butter, cheese, and yogurt, but ultra-heat treatment (UHT) milk, where the milk is very briefly heated to 265–300°F, is not suitable for cheese making because the process affects the nature of the proteins within the milk.

Cow's milk is by far the most widely available milk. The revival of artisanal cheese making in the West has stimulated a renewed interest in reviving traditional breeds of dairy cows noted for the quality and flavor of their milk, such as Brown Swiss cows in the United States and Ayrshires in Britain. The milk from Jersey cows contains 5.2% fat (as opposed to the 3.6% fat found in Holstein Friesians) and is a deep yellow color with a rich, creamy flavor. The milk is much valued for cream and butter making, but the size of the fat globules makes it tricky for producing cheese. Cow's milk is sold in a range of fat contents, from skim to whole, allowing for experimentation when it comes to making dairy products at home.

Many people with a lactic intolerance prefer to consume dairy products made from sheep's milk or goat's milk. In both of these milks, the fat globules are not only far smaller than in cow's milk but also more evenly dispersed (i.e. naturally homogenized), which makes them more digestible.

Bright white sheep's milk is very high in fats and proteins, which means that there is a high yield of cheese from the milk. The milk has a distinctive nutty flavor, which also often characterizes the cheese and yogurt made from it. Goat's milk, also bright white, has a subtle but distinctive flavor, which distinguishes dairy products made from it. Buffalo milk, which is rarely offered on sale to the public, is a brilliant white milk highly valued by cheese makers because its high fat and protein content allow for a very good yield of cheese from the milk. The most famous cheese made from buffalo milk is mozzarella.

How to store

Keeping your homemade dairy products cool is essential. Butter, soft cheeses, and yogurt should all be stored in the refrigerator, either in containers or well wrapped to prevent them from becoming tainted by other foods: butter will keep for several weeks; soft cheeses for 1–2 weeks, and yogurt for 2 weeks. Butter can be frozen for up to eight months.

Left: A Jersey cow
Right: Whole cow's milk used in the yogurt recipe on page 22

Making yogurt

This recipe uses whole cow's milk, but you can substitute lower-fat cow's milk or use other milks such as goat's or sheep's. In order to trigger the fermentation process, you need to add "live" yogurt, which will be labeled as such on the tub. The yogurt needs to be incubated in a warm spot, such as an insulated cooler box in which you place a couple of sealed jars of freshly boiled water in order to raise the temperature.

3⅜ cups whole milk
3 tablespoons "live" yogurt

Equipment needed
cheese-making thermometer
large sterilized jar or
small sterilized jars

Makes 2½ cups

1 Assemble all the ingredients and equipment.

2 Place the milk in a heavy-based pan. Heat the milk gently until it reaches 185°F, checking it with the thermometer. Remove from direct heat and allow to cool for 10–15 minutes until the temperature reduces to 110°F. Now mix the "live" yogurt into the warm milk.

3 Carefully pour the mixture into a sterilized jar or jars. Cover and set aside to incubate in a warm place for 7–8 hours until set to your taste. Store in the refrigerator for up to a week. This is delicious served with honey (see main picture).

Making cream cheese

The simplest way to start making cheese at home is by making a soft cheese. This can be made very simply indeed by draining yogurt through cheesecloth. Alternately, you can curdle warm milk using lemon juice or rennet, then drain the curds in muslin or cheesecloth to create a soft cheese. Should you be bitten by the cheese-making bug, you'll find it worthwhile buying a few pieces of equipment, such as a cheese-making thermometer and some muslin for draining, and also some cheese-making rennet. Thanks to the Internet, it's now very easy to track down specialist mail-order cheese-making companies to supply you. Many of these also offer starter packs of bacterial cultures to help you create specific cheeses, such as goat cheese or mozzarella. As its name suggests, the soft cheese we are making here is made from milk enriched with cream.

2½ cups whole milk

1⅝ cups heavy cream

⅜ rounded cup "live" yogurt

5 drops of cheese-making rennet, dissolved in a little water that has been boiled and cooled

salt

Equipment needed

cheese-making thermometer

colander

large square of muslin or cheesecloth

Makes 7–10 oz., depending on how long it drains for (7 oz. being after overnight draining)

1 Mix together the milk, heavy cream and yogurt in a large, heavy-based pan. Gently heat this mixture until it reaches 100°F, testing with the thermometer. Remove from direct heat and stir in the rennet mixture. Stir for 2–3 minutes, during which time the milk mixture will begin to curdle. Cover and set aside to stand for 1 hour until the curd has set.

2 Using a shallow, slotted spoon, cut through the mixture, right down to the bottom of the pan, at roughly 1-in. intervals in both directions. This helps the curds to separate from the whey, allowing more liquid to stay in the pan when you transfer the curds to the muslin (see step 4). Leave to stand for another 20 minutes.

4 Put the curds into a muslin-lined colander standing on a deep plate. Gather up the muslin and squeeze the curds to encourage the whey to drain off through the muslin. (The curds need to drain for at least 8 hours, so you will need to tie the muslin up and suspend it over the colander. A longer drainage produces a denser-textured cheese.)

3 Using the same spoon, carefully remove the curds from the pan, allowing the whey to drain back into the pan.

5 Season the cream cheese with salt, adding only a little at a time and mixing thoroughly. Store, covered, in the refrigerator for up to two weeks.

Making butter

Making your own butter is very easy and requires no specialist equipment (though if you can get hold of butter hands, you will be able to form the butter into the traditional blocks). Unsalted butter keeps for only a few days, but adding salt allows the butter to be kept for a couple of weeks, covered, in the refrigerator.

1¼ cups heavy cream, at room temperature

⅜ cup very cold water

salt

Equipment needed

food processor fitted with metal cutting blades

sieve

potato masher

Makes 4½ oz.

1 Place the cream in the food processor and blend for a few minutes until the cream separates into pale yellow butter and a milky-white liquid, which is the buttermilk. Using the sieve, drain off the buttermilk, reserving this for drinking or for using in cooking. You need to now remove any buttermilk remaining in the butter; otherwise it will turn rancid and taint the butter.

2 Return the butter to the food processor and add the cold water. Blend, then drain off the cloudy liquid. Repeat this process four times, until the liquid running off is practically clear.

3 Transfer the butter to a large bowl and work by mashing with a potato masher to bring the butter together and to press out any remaining water, draining it off as it comes out. Season the butter with salt to taste and work with the masher until the butter is smooth and firm, with no more water coming out when worked.

4 Transfer the butter to a ramekin or a mold or simply shape with a spoon. Cut into pats to serve. To store the butter, wrap in waxed paper to prevent it from being tainted by smells from other foods. Keep in the refrigerator.

Making buttermilk

Buttermilk, as its name suggests, was historically a by-product of making butter, the white, milky liquid produced when the butterfat comes together. Nowadays, however, most commercially produced buttermilk is made by adding a culture to milk to ferment it, then stirring the resulting curd to make a thick, smooth liquid with a sour tang. A quick and simple way of making buttermilk at home is to sour milk by adding vinegar or lemon juice.

1 Assemble the ingredients.

2 Place the room-temperature milk in a bowl. Add the lemon juice or white wine vinegar.

2 cups whole milk, at room temperature

2 tablespoons lemon juice or white wine vinegar

Makes 2 cups buttermilk

3 Stir to mix well together. Leave to stand for 15 minutes, during which time the milk will thicken slightly and take on a faintly sour tang. Store covered in the refrigerator, where it will keep for up to a week, and stir before serving.

Using your produce

Cream of cauliflower soup

This is a particularly creamy soup adapted from a French recipe. Originally, it was thickened by beating in egg yolks, but I have found that the buttermilk gives it a lighter touch. Make sure that you use a firm, fresh cauliflower, as once they go soft, cauliflowers tend to turn slightly bitter and so ruin the flavor of the soup.

I large firm cauliflower

3 cups stock (chicken or vegetable)

pinch of nutmeg

salt, to taste

1¼ cups buttermilk (see page 28)

Serves 4—6

1 Clean the cauliflower, remove the outer leaves, and break up into small pieces or florets. Cook these in lightly salted boiling water until soft. Drain and add the cooking water to the stock.

2 Pound the cauliflower to a purée and return it to the saucepan. Pour in the stock, and add a pinch of nutmeg, and extra salt if necessary. Simmer for about 15 minutes and then remove from the heat.

3 Allow the soup to cool, and then pour in the buttermilk, beating vigorously with a balloon whisk. Gently reheat, taking great care that the soup does not boil and so curdle the buttermilk.

Beef in buttermilk

The Austrians have a particular method of dealing with poor-quality beef. They marinate it in buttermilk, sharpened with capers and lemon rind, and then bake it slowly in a clay pot.

1¼ cups buttermilk (see page 28)

2 medium onions, minced

I teaspoon capers

I garlic clove

grated rind of I lemon

3–4½ lb. beef (any cheap cut)

salt and pepper, to taste

Equipment needed

clay pot

Serves 4—6

1 Preheat the oven to 400°F. Prepare the clay pot by soaking it in water for 15 minutes.

2 Mix the buttermilk with onion, capers, garlic, and lemon rind and pour over the beef. Leave the meat to soak up the flavor for a minimum of four hours, turning it occasionally in the marinade.

3 Put the beef and marinade into the prepared clay pot. Cover and bake in the oven for two hours. Remove the lid and allow the meat to brown and cook for another 20 minutes.

4 When cooked, carve the meat into thin slices and arrange on a dish. Strain the onion and liquidize with the capers to form a purée. Skim the gravy to remove the fat and reduce to half the quantity. Stir into the purée and pour over the sliced meat.

Beet, goat cheese, and pine nut salad with melba toast

This salad has a wintry, festive sumptuousness, thanks to the deep red of the beets and the bright white of the homemade cheese.

1½ lb. small, unpeeled beets, trimmed

12 slices white bread

1 lb. total mixed salad leaves (about 20 cups, torn into small pieces)

½ lb. crumbly goat cheese

1 cup pine nuts, toasted in a dry skillet

bunch of basil

2 garlic cloves, chopped

5 tablespoons olive oil

freshly squeezed juice of 2 lemons

coarse sea salt and freshly ground black pepper

Serves 12

1 Preheat the oven to 350°F. Put the beets into a roasting pan and roast in the oven for 45 minutes. Remove from the oven, leave to cool, then peel and quarter.

2 Meanwhile, to make the melba toast, toast the slices of bread, then remove the crusts. Using a large, sharp knife, split each piece of toast through the middle, to give two whole slices of toast with one soft bread side each. Cut in half diagonally, then cook under a preheated broiler, soft side up, until golden and curled. Watch the toasts carefully, as they can burn quickly.

3 Put the mixed leaves onto a big serving dish, add the beets, crumble the goat cheese on top, then sprinkle with pine nuts and torn basil leaves.

4 Put the garlic, oil, and lemon juice into a small bowl or jar. Add salt and pepper, mix well, then pour over the salad. Serve with the melba toast.

Baked sea bream

Yogurt has a tendency to curdle when boiled or baked, so it is advisable to stabilize it before cooking. To save time, you can stabilize a large amount and keep in the fridge for a week or so.

To stabilize the yogurt

2 cups yogurt (see page 22)

I egg white, lightly beaten

pinch of salt

I sea bream, I½–2 lb., cleaned, gutted, and descaled

I teaspoon coriander seeds

2 cloves garlic

6 peppercorns

I teaspoon coarse sea salt

I onion, minced

grated rind and juice of I lemon

Equipment needed

terracotta oven pot

Serves 4

1 Preheat the oven to 350°F. Beat the yogurt in a saucepan and stir in the egg white and pinch of salt. Gently bring to the boil, stirring constantly, with a regular action, and then simmer for about 10 minutes on very low heat, as the yogurt must not be allowed to burn. The yogurt will form a smooth thick paste, which can be added to meat or vegetables and reheated without fear of curdling or separating.

2 Prepare the terracotta pot by soaking it in water for 15 minutes.

3 Crush the coriander seeds and garlic with the peppercorns and salt, and mix the paste with the onion and lemon rind.

4 Lay the fish in the prepared pot and spread the mixture all over the fish. Pour the lemon juice over. Place the pot in the oven and bake for an hour.

5 When the fish is cooked, lift it onto a serving dish and keep warm. Pour the juice into the yogurt. Stir vigorously. Heat gently until almost boiling. Pour over the fish and serve immediately.

Wild mushroom and butter bean soup

Believe it or not, this soup is best made with dried wild mushrooms. To dry your mushrooms, just cut them into slices, spread them out on a wire rack, and leave them in the oven on the lowest possible setting for at least 6 hours. But if you are not the hunter-gatherer type who has picked their own, simply buy a package.

I oz. dried wild mushrooms

2 tablespoons olive oil

I onion, sliced

2 garlic cloves, crushed

3 cups butter (dried lima) beans, soaked overnight in water

⅝ cup full-fat yogurt (see page 22)

coarse sea salt and freshly ground black pepper

2 tablespoons butter (see page 26)

parsley, chopped (optional)

Equipment needed:

muslin-lined sieve

hand blender or food processor

Serves 4–6

1 Put the mushrooms in a suitable bowl, pour over them about 1½ cups boiling water, and leave to soak for about 30 minutes or until the mushrooms are quite soft. Using a slotted spoon lift out the mushrooms and refresh them by putting them in a clean bowl with just enough cold water to cover. Reserve the water in which the mushrooms have been soaking, but if it looks particularly gritty, strain it through a muslin-lined sieve. Otherwise, just leave it, as a few particles will not do any harm; actually they will probably enhance the flavor of the soup.

2 In a large saucepan heat the olive oil, add the onion and garlic, and cook gently over moderate heat to soften for about 5–7 minutes. Drain the beans and add to the saucepan, stirring with a wooden spoon until they are well coated with the olive oil. Then pour in 3 cups water and the water in which the mushrooms have been soaking, gently bring to the boil, and simmer for about 90 minutes or until the beans are softened.

3 Using either a hand blender or food processor, blitz the soup until it is smooth. Return to the pan, stir in the yogurt, adjust the seasoning, and gently reheat. If you like your soup with a bit of texture, keep a few whole butter beans back before you purée the soup, then stir them in with the yogurt.

4 Meanwhile, melt the butter in a suitable sauté pan. Squeeze the mushrooms with your hands until they are dry, and roughly chop them into small pieces. Add the mushrooms to the pan and sauté gently over medium heat for 5 minutes or until they are tender. Stir the mushrooms into the soup, adjust the seasoning and, if you think the soup needs a little color, sprinkle some chopped parsley on top just before serving.

Buttermilk cornbread

Stoneground yellow cornmeal gives this cornbread a wonderful texture, and the buttermilk and honey make for a soft, sweet crumb. For a change, you could add 3 tablespoons toasted pine nuts, fresh or frozen corn kernels, or grated sharp cheese.

1 cup fine yellow cornmeal, preferably stoneground

⅞ cup all-purpose flour

1½ teaspoons baking powder

½ teaspoon baking soda

½ teaspoon coarse sea salt

1 large egg

3 tablespoons plus 1 teaspoon unsalted butter, melted

3 tablespoons honey

1 scant cup buttermilk (see page 28)

Equipment needed:

8-in. square cake pan, well greased

Makes 1 medium loaf (6–8 portions)

1 Preheat the oven to 400°F. Put the cornmeal, flour, baking powder, baking soda, and salt in a large bowl and stir with a wooden spoon until the ingredients are thoroughly mixed.

2 In a separate bowl, beat the egg with the melted butter, honey, and buttermilk. Stir into the dry ingredients to make a thick, smooth batter.

3 Transfer the mixture to the prepared pan and spread evenly.

4 Bake for 15–20 minutes until golden and a toothpick inserted into the center comes out clean. Turn out onto a bread board, cut into large squares, and serve warm.

This is best eaten the same day. Can be frozen for up to a month—gently warm before serving.

Summer berry frozen yogurt

Use full-fat homemade yogurt for this recipe and you will be rewarded with a delectable dessert. Low-fat yogurt can give an unpleasant, icy texture.

4 cups mixed summer berries, such as strawberries, blackberries, and raspberries

⅝ cup superfine sugar

2 cups full-fat yogurt (see page 22)

Equipment needed:

food processor

fine-meshed nylon sieve

an ice cream machine (optional)

Serves 4

1 Warm the berries and sugar in a saucepan over low heat for several minutes, until the fruit begins to release its juices. Transfer to a food processor and blend to a purée. Push the purée through a fine-meshed nylon sieve to remove the seeds. Stir in the yogurt.

2 Churn in an ice cream machine (if available) until almost frozen. Transfer to a freezerproof container and freeze until ready to serve. Alternatively, you can make the frozen yogurt without a machine. The mixture should be frozen in a shallow container. When almost solid, beat it well with a wire whisk or electric beater until smooth, then return to the freezer. Repeat the process twice more, to break down the ice crystals, and the result will be smooth and silky.

3 Transfer the frozen yogurt to the refrigerator for 20–30 minutes before serving, to let it soften evenly throughout.

4 Homemade frozen yogurt is best eaten as soon as possible after being made, and certainly within a week.

Thin crackers

These crackers bear absolutely no relation to plain
store-bought crackers, as they are far crisper and have a
far more interesting taste. However, they have a short
shelf-life and should really be eaten on the day they are
made. If you do want to keep them, put them in a tin
while still warm along with a sheet of waxed paper to
prevent them from going soggy. You can always revive
them by warming them briefly in the oven.

1⅝ cups white bread flour

large pinch of salt

1 teaspoon baking powder

3 tablespoons plus 2 teaspoons butter (see page 26),
cut into small pieces

6 tablespoons light cream

ground sea salt, for sprinkling

Makes 15–20

1 Preheat the oven to 350°F. Generously grease a baking sheet
with butter.

2 Sift the flour into a bowl with the salt and baking powder. Add
the butter and cut it into the flour with a knife. Then rub it in lightly
with the fingertips, until it is the texture of fine breadcrumbs. Stir in
the cream, then gather the mixture together to make a firm dough,
adding a tablespoon of water if necessary.

3 On a lightly floured flat surface, roll the dough out very thinly,
pressing down quite hard on it. Using a 3-in. cookie cutter, cut
into rounds. Arrange the crackers on the prepared baking sheet,
prick them all over with a fork, and sprinkle a little sea salt on
top. Bake in the preheated oven for 10–15 minutes, or until
golden brown. Turn out on wire racks and leave to cool.

Fruit kabobs

You can use slices of any firm fruit—apples,
pineapples, or plums—or strawberries or blackberries
for a fruit kabob. And you can vary the flavor of the
butter by using a different alcohol, such as brandy,
whisky, or gin, or by adding a handful of freshly
chopped mint or a pinch of chopped almonds
or walnuts.

1½ cups strawberries

4 large apricots, cut into thick wedges

3 tablespoons unsalted butter (see page 26)

1 tablespoon brown sugar

1 tablespoon rum

Serves 4

1 Preheat the broiler.

2 Thread the fruit on four individual wooden or metal skewers,
alternating the strawberries with the apricot wedges. If the berries
are very large, cut them in half, but do not bother to hull them.

3 Blitz the butter with the brown sugar in a blender and, with the
machine still running, pour in the rum. Using a pastry brush, paint
the fruit all over with the flavored butter. Broil for about a minute
on each side or for just long enough to melt the butter and heat
the fruit.

Tip: If you need to wash the strawberries, do so with a little
red or white wine, rather than water. It will help the fruit stay
firm and enhance the flavor.

Chapter 2

THE BAKERY

The foods we make from flour and bake in the oven play a very significant part in our lives. Bread, in particular, is one of the most fundamental of our foods, an everyday staple, yet one that also has a symbolic and spiritual resonance. One has only to think of those words from the Lord's Prayer, "Give us this day our daily bread" or the expression "breaking bread" to realize that this is a foodstuff that has historically held a very special place in our lives. Flour, enriched with fat and eggs and sweetened with sugar, is also the base of treats such as cookies, cakes, and pastries. Baking a cake is still the way in which we mark special occasions, such as birthdays and weddings.

There is something about baking at home, the process by which a few ordinary ingredients—flour, a raising agent such as yeast or baking powder, water, fat, and sugar—are transformed into breads, pastries, cakes, and cookies, that is not only profoundly satisfying but also an easy way of reconnecting to a timeless tradition, with family recipes passed down through the generations.

Bread

The history of bread dates back to prehistoric times, when flatbreads made from a paste of crushed grains mixed with water were cooked on stones or embers. The story of bread is inevitably closely tied to the very early days of human agriculture and the cultivation of grains, including wheat, which first took place in Western Asia before 7000 B.C.E. The ancient Egyptians cultivated grains, and the earliest archaeological evidence of leavened bread (bread created using a raising agent) comes from Egypt c.4000 B.C.E. The process of leavening probably first came about naturally, because in a warm climate wild yeasts would be attracted to a grain paste and would then set to work.

Grinding the grain to make flour for bread was, for centuries, a long and labor-intensive process. It began with the use of

grinding stones and led to the rise of windmills and watermills, which turned huge millstones to grind the grain. The nineteenth-century roller mill, in which multiple steel rollers ground the grain, allowed white flour to be produced quickly and efficiently, and sold cheaply. Since Roman times, bread made from refined white flour had been an exclusive food, the preserve of the wealthy, but the new roller mills and mechanization put an end to that. Today, most flours are produced through roller milling, with only a handful of craft millers using traditional grinding stones to produce their flour.

It was during the twentieth century that baking underwent a major change, moving from the traditional methods used by small bakeries toward industrialized ones suitable for large-scale plant bakeries. The slow rising of dough was replaced by processes using accelerated dough development, which required the addition of chemical "improvers," preservatives, and emulsifiers to the flour, and a speeded-up process of intense mechanical agitation. Most bread today is produced using these methods, although in many countries craft bakers are still able to find a niche market.

Pastry

Flour is, of course, the base not only of bread but also of pastry (and to a lesser extent cakes and cookies). Making pastry (including piecrust) from a mixture of flour, fat, and liquid has long been considered a separate craft from baking bread. There are many types of pastry, from fine phyllo pastry, thought to have originated with the Turks and used in layers in pastries such as sweet baklava, to egg-rich choux pastry, used by the French in creations such as éclairs or cream puffs, and buttery, flaky pastry, used to top potpies. Pastry's continued primary use is as a container for other ingredients, whether an apple pie, a mushroom vol-au-vent, or a Cornish pasty (in which the crimped edge traditionally formed a "handle" to hold the pasty by, so that dirty hands didn't touch the filling). In medieval times, pastry cases called "coffers" were made to encase and protect foods such as meat.

Left: The trademark slits on a French baguette help the escape of steam and carbon dioxide
Right: A bakery usually makes more than one type of product, so that it can supply customers with a range of both sweet and savory items

Flour

The starting point for bread and pastry is flour, with all good bakers stressing the importance of using good-quality flour and, most importantly, the right flour for the job. Most flour is made from wheat, which is valued above other grains for its high gluten content; gluten molecules stretch and hold their shape, so that the bread rises successfully. Nowadays, the most widely grown species of wheat for bread making is *Triticum aestivum*. It has several cultivars, and those with a high gluten content are known as "hard" wheats (which produce a "strong" flour suitable for bread and pasta).

Flour is also made from other grains, such as maize, buckwheat, or rye, and there is a renewed interest in ancient grains, such as spelt, used by the Romans, or kamut, a grain grown by the Egyptians. Flour from these grains is increasingly available to the home baker. There are also flours made from nuts and legumes, such as gram flour from chickpeas.

As you can see from the list, there are many different types of flour. To make a leavened bread (that is, one that rises), you need flour with a high gluten content, sometimes called "strong," but when you're making pies or cakes, less gluten is needed, as you want a soft, yielding texture rather than a tough one.

Different types of flour

All-purpose flour Also called plain flour, this is the most commonly used kind of flour. It has been milled and sieved to extract the bran and wheat germ; bleached versions have slightly less protein than unbleached. Enriched all-purpose has iron and B-vitamins added.

Bran The hard outer layer of a cereal grain that is removed during the milling process.

Bread flour Sometimes called strong flour, it has a high protein content, which forms gluten when moistened; this helps the bread to rise. It comes in white and wholewheat forms.

Brown flour Popular in Britain, this flour typically contains 85 percent of the original bran and wheat germ, and usually some malt; Granary bread is a well-known brand.

Buckwheat flour This is gluten-free, so suitable for people with celiac disease. It has a nutty flavor and is often used in pancakes.

Cake flour Very finely milled white flour with a low gluten content, used to give cakes a higher rise and finer texture.

Self-rising flour A white flour that has had a raising agent, such as baking powder, added to it.

Stone ground flour Flour that has been milled in a traditional way, by grinding the grain with millstones, instead of metal rollers, so that the elements of the grain—the bran, wheat germ, and endosperm—are crushed together.

Wholemeal flour As its name suggests, this flour is made by grinding up whole wheat kernels with nothing removed.

Left: Freshly milled flour
Opposite: Use the heel of your hands when kneading

Meet the producer: Staff of Life

A love of baking ever since he was a boy saw Simon Thomas, together with his wife Julie, set up Staff of Life bakery in England's Lake District in 1997. They produce a range of handmade breads and cakes from locally produced flour.

"Ingredients are key to my baking," states Simon. "In flour I look for a combination of flavor and gluten protein, choosing the flour according to the bread we want to make. So for our classic wholemeal, I use a mix of Salkeld Watermill flour, which is very flavorful and coarse, together with flour from Carr's Mills, who make very consistent flour, for strength. Our bread is ultra-low in salt, under one percent of sea salt, so that rather than just tasting salt, the taste of the grain itself comes through. Our spelt loaf, for example, has a deep caramel flavor to it that comes from the spelt."

To raise his breads, Simon uses Fermipan dried yeast and, intriguingly, a homemade elderflower-based sourdough starter, carrying over some of the dough each time he makes sourdough to use it to start the next batch. "There's a natural yeast on elderflowers, which is far stronger than baker's yeast and works beautifully," he explains. "Because it's so strong, we use a low ratio of starter to flour, 10 percent rather than the normal 20 percent, which makes our sourdough less sour. Lots of people buy it who normally don't like sourdough."

Having made the dough, Simon allows for a long, slow gentle first rising, followed by shorter second and sometimes a third rising. "Our bread is made very slowly. Our doughs all rise for a minimum of 15 hours, and a lot of them have two days' rising. The time gives a lot of flavor and makes the dough easy to handle. It's a soft dough, so you don't have to punch at it, instead you knead it gently; persuasion rather than confrontation." The bread is baked in a

professional electric oven. "Each batch bakes differently so I keep a close eye on it. It gets so I can tell when it's ready by the smell."

Of the bread-making process, Simon observes, "It's a bit like training animals: every dough has its own character. Some mornings you can touch the dough and know that it's going to make fantastic bread today. Making bread is an easily acquired skill. I run bread-making courses, and there's an expression people get on their faces when they've got it; the same expression that someone gets when they realize how simple a magic trick really is."

Yeast and other raising agents

In order for bread to rise, it needs to have a raising agent added to the dough. Nowadays, yeast is the best known of these agents. When given the right conditions, yeast works within a loaf of bread by multiplying fast and creating bubbles of carbon dioxide, so causing the bread to rise. One yeast species in particular, *Saccharomyces cerevisiae*, which is widely used in baking, is valued for its reliability as a raising agent and its lack of a pronounced flavor, thereby allowing the flavor of the flour to shine through. It is this species that is available commercially in a number of forms: compressed, dry (or active dry), and rapid-rising (or quick-rising).

Compressed yeast, also known as cake yeast or fresh yeast, is sold in the form of a soft, moist cake, which crumbles easily. Many craft bakers will use only compressed yeast, feeling that it gives a slower rise and creates bread with a better flavor. Dry yeast, which comes in granular form, is a dried, dormant form of fresh yeast, requiring immersion in warm water to activate it before being added to the dough. Rapid-rising yeast, also in granular form, does not require a separate immersion in warm water to activate it and can simply be sprinkled dry into the flour. It is made from a very fast-acting strain of *Saccharomyces cerevisiae*, so grows very vigorously, creating carbon dioxide quickly.

While compressed yeast can be tricky to source, dry and rapid-rising are widely available. Because of their concentrated nature, dry yeasts are more powerful than compressed yeast, and so less is needed to raise the dough. If substituting yeasts, a general rule of thumb is to substitute half the amount of dry yeast for the amount of compressed yeast and one-quarter the amount of rapid-rising yeast for the amount of compressed yeast.

Sourdough starters are the most traditional way of raising bread. These are created by encouraging the fermentation of wild yeasts naturally present in the atmosphere in a piece of dough or a batter. Using a commercially produced *Saccharomyces cerevisiae* yeast to create a sourdough starter does not work because the process of making sourdough requires wild yeasts, often from the genus *Candida*, to dominate. Once made, a portion of this sourdough, rich in wild yeasts, is mixed into the dough to cause it to rise. Sourdough starters need to be looked after and "fed" to keep them active. They are perpetuated by keeping back a portion of the dough to use for the next batch. Many craft bakers have carefully nurtured sourdoughs that trace their origins back for many years. Although a sour tang is a characteristic flavor of bread made using sourdough, because populations of wild yeasts vary from place to place, sourdoughs range in flavor according to region; for example, a San Francisco sourdough loaf will taste different from a French *pain au levain*. Another characteristic of using a sourdough starter is that the dough will take longer to rise than one made from commercial yeast.

Creating the right environment for the yeast to grow in is important, with yeast needing moisture, food, and warmth. When making bread, liquid (usually just water) is added to the flour to create the dough. Flours vary in their ability to absorb water, so it should be added gradually. Yeast's favorite food is sugar, which is why sugar is often used in recipes for bread dough. At low temperatures, yeasts become dormant, but at higher temperatures, they can die; the optimum temperature for yeasts to grow in is around 79°F. Having made your dough with yeast and provided it with moisture and food in the form of water and sugar, you should then set the dough aside to rest and rise in a warm, draft-free place.

Other raising agents used in baking are chemical raisers such as baking of soda, which works when combined with acid elements such as buttermilk or a sourdough culture. Baking powder contains both baking soda and an acid element.

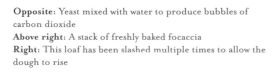

Opposite: Yeast mixed with water to produce bubbles of carbon dioxide
Above right: A stack of freshly baked focaccia
Right: This loaf has been slashed multiple times to allow the dough to rise

Pastry

As a general rule, pastry, including piecrust, is made from a mixture of flour, fat, and water. There are a number of types of pastry—such as piecrust, puff, choux, and phyllo—with the differences arising from how they are made and the ingredients used. The fat can be rubbed into the flour with your fingertips, as with piecrust, or layered in the dough and then rolled out, as with puff pastry.

Piecrust, classically made with a ratio of half the weight of fat to flour, then bound together with a little water or beaten egg, is widely used for both sweet and savory baking. There are many versions of piecrust, made with differing ratios of fat to flour and different fats. Butter, for example, gives a buttery richness to the piecrust. Vegetable shortening is often used and is suitable for both sweet and savory crust. Lard is still valued by some bakers for the melting texture it gives to pastry, though it is seldom used in American kitchens today. Pastry can be sweetened or flavored with ingredients such as cocoa, peanuts, or vanilla, making it an extremely versatile foodstuff.

Above left: Almond croissants are made from a leavened variant of puff pastry and rolled to form their distinctive crescent shape
Left: Perennial breakfast favorite, the *pain au chocolat*
Opposite: Olive and rosemary focaccia

Meet the producer: Richard Bertinet

An eloquent champion of real bread, French baker Richard Bertinet is noted not only for his range of fine breads but also for his ability to teach bread and pastry making (as he does in Bath, England)—an aspect of his work he finds deeply rewarding.

He has a very clear idea of how to make bread. "To start with, you need a good dough to make good bread. I use a higher ratio of water to flour in my dough than most people, so around 500g [2⅛ cups] of water to 1kg [7 cups] of good strong bread flour. People are scared of sticky dough; they find it messy. To me it's normal, it's not sticky. So many people add flour to the surface or sprinkle it over the dough as they work it. You don't want to do that, as you're changing the ratio of flour to water. I use a fresh yeast from France, L'Hirondelle, the same one I've used for many years. It's beautiful to use. I use as little yeast as possible. Dried yeast to me is too powerful."

Richard's distinctive kneading method is central to how he makes bread. Rather than pushing the dough with palms and knuckles, he lifts the dough in the air, up and over on itself, then slaps it down on the surface, working the dough in this way until, after a few minutes, it becomes elastic and supple. "There is a technique to it," he cautions. "It must be done carefully. It's not about bashing the dough. You don't need to be strong, but you must use your whole body. Kneading the dough the way I do adds in air," he explains, "and makes a light loaf. Nobody wants to make a heavy, dense loaf."

When it comes to making pastry, a common mistake in Richard's view is rough handling. "Overworking the pastry is very common. You need to be gentle and it's very important to let it rest enough. A bit of planning is important when it comes to pastry. Be patient; don't be scared. People come on my course very scared of making pastry; we teach them how to make it and how to roll it and when they leave, the fear factor has gone."

The bread oven

The ancient Egyptians are usually credited with the invention of enclosed ovens in which to bake bread. In order to preserve precious fuel, there has been a long tradition in many societies of communal baking, with the baker's oven often being used by other members of the village, too. Today, a number of artisanal bakeries continue to use traditional wood-fired ovens, in which the bread is placed straight on the preheated stones of the oven floor. Bread lovers appreciate the particular texture these ovens give to both the crust and the base of the bread.

In these days of gas and electricity, however, most domestic cooks don't have access to a wood-fired oven. While gas and electric ovens work well for baking cakes, cookies, and pies, they are less successful when it comes to creating a good crust on loaves of bread. One useful tip to recreate the effect of a wood-fired oven is to invest in stone or ceramic baking tiles or pizza stones, which retain heat very effectively. These should be preheated in the oven, then the bread placed directly on the hot stone and baked in the oven.

Many professional bakeries also use steam in their ovens to create a moist atmosphere in order to help the bread rise successfully. Tips for the home baker to replicate this include spraying your loaf with water before you bake it; spraying the walls of the hot oven once you've placed the loaf inside; placing a metal tray with hot water in the oven; or dropping ice cubes on the floor of the oven.

Above: A wood-fired oven will maintain heat for several hours after the fire has died
Right: Long Crichel use a traditonal wood-burning oven

Meet the producer: Long Crichel

Jamie and Rose Campbell set up Long Crichel Bakery in 2000 with a very clear idea of what they wanted.

"The rules we made for ourselves were [that] our bread would be organic, made by hand, drawing on traditional techniques, and baked in a wood-burning oven," explains Jamie. "We were also interested in sourdough, which, given we're in Dorset, was very rare at the time. We started making our wheat sourdough using grapes from the vine growing on the house. It's all about harvesting wild yeasts, creating an environment for them to grow in. Bread is a product of fermentation."

An eye to fine-quality ingredients is matched by attention to method. "As a commercial bakery one has to be consistent," points out Jamie. "Our dough is quite wet. We have a house way of kneading, which is to knead as little as we can get away with; we don't want to overwork the dough. The more you knead, the finer your crumb is, so we'll adjust our kneading accordingly. A fine-crumbed bread will require more kneading than a country-style loaf, which has larger bubbles inside it." Long, slow fermentation is key to the "depth of flavor" that Jamie looks for in the bakery's breads. "We create what's perceived to be a typical English loaf: light, with a fine crumb. To make this we use the overnight sponge method, working with a fermented dough, which rises and collapses. This gives body and flavor. We don't want something light and insipid. Another one of our signature breads is the malted five seed bread: a sourdough loaf made with long fermentation of around 20 hours, which has a fantastic flavor."

The magnificent, large wood-fired oven, which burns wood thinned from the trees on the big estate around them, is central to the bakery's distinctive style. "Even though bread, in one way, is so simple," comments Jamie, "there are a huge number of variations and the baking of it is one of them. Having a wood-fired oven really does make a difference. Bakers say the best way to bake bread is with heat that's falling. You make the fire in the oven, then you close it down and allow the heat to distribute evenly. It does make a difference to the quality of the crust. We add steam to the atmosphere using a water feed, which vaporizes. A hot, moist atmosphere allows the bread to be elastic and soft, open up, and rise more smoothly."

Sourcing the ingredients

Talk to any baker and they will recommend finding a flour that works well for you. Bear in mind that small-scale craft millers produce flours that often have a lot of flavor but can be tricky for novice bakers to use because their gluten content may vary from batch to batch. Similarly, experiment with different types of yeast, including wild yeast sourdough, to see which you enjoy using.

How to store

All flour has a limited shelf life, with wholewheat flour deteriorating faster than white because of the presence of wheat germ. Store flour in a cool, dry place. Alternatively, wrap it well in plastic wrap or place it in a plastic container and freeze it; frozen flour will last from six months to a year.

When it comes to yeast, compressed yeast deteriorates easily and should be stored in the refrigerator and used quickly. Alternatively, if you buy a large amount, cut it into 1-oz. pieces, wrap them, and store them in the freezer, where they will keep for up to six months. Dry and rapid-rising yeasts, though less perishable than compressed, go stale with time and become less effective. Buy them in small amounts, store in an airtight container in a cool, dry place, and use them up quickly.

When it comes to keeping baked goods, they should be allowed to cool, then be covered and stored in a cool, dry place. In order to keep their texture for as long as possible, store cookies in an airtight container. Bread and pastry, including piecrust, freeze well.

Left: Fresh yeast mixed with water, ready to be combined with flour and salt to produce dough
Right: Flat, wooden implements, known as "peels," are used to place bread in and out of the oven

Techniques

While a certain mystique has grown up about baking bread and pastry, the reality is that these can both be made very successfully in the home. The are several key processes that may at first seem tricky, but do remember that, as with many culinary skills, the more you do something, the simpler it becomes.

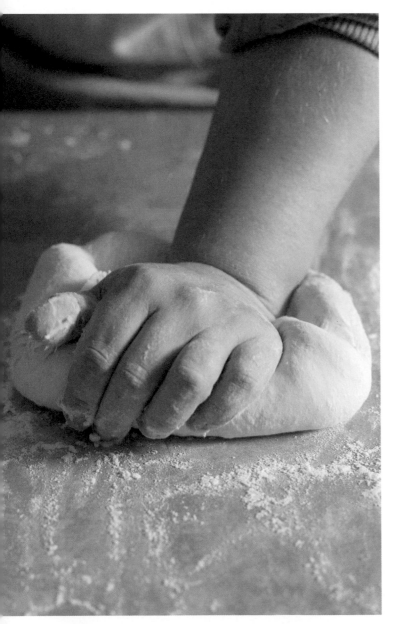

Kneading bread dough

An intrinsic part of making bread is kneading: the process by which the dough is worked in order to develop the gluten inside the flour, making it elastic enough to rise successfully. There are many different schools of thought on how to knead; some people advocate stretching and pushing the dough on a work surface, while others (see page 45) advocate lifting up the dough and folding it over on itself. A dough-scraper, to gather the dough together and clean it off your hands, is a rather useful piece of equipment.

Whichever kneading method you choose, experienced bakers agree that starting with a soft dough, rather than a firm, dry one, is best. Use a warm surface to knead on, such as a wooden table, because a cold surface like marble will make the dough too cool. Avoid adding extra flour to the work surface or to your dough, as this will simply make your bread too dry. As you work the dough, you're looking for it to change texture, taking on a smooth, pliable, elastic quality. Once the dough has been kneaded, it should be loosely covered with a damp dish towel or plastic wrap and placed in a warm, draft-free spot until doubled in size.

Left: If dough is not kneaded for long enough it will collapse, creating a dense, unappetizing bread
Right: Bakers use a lame, a double-sized cutting tool, to slash their loaves prior to putting them in the oven

Shaping bread

When it comes to shaping bread, there are a number of ways to go about it and many shapes to choose from. Proofing baskets, also known as bannetons, are designed to shape the dough as it rises or "proves." Dough can also be set aside to rise, then shaped as desired, either freeform or by using bread pans.

Slashing the bread is done not only for decorative purposes but also to allow the dough to expand correctly. Make sure you use a very sharp knife to slash the dough.

Making pastry/piecrust

When it comes to making and handling pastry, it is important to keep it cool because of its fat content. If the fat begins to melt, the pastry will be oily and difficult to handle. A piece of naturally cool marble is a traditional surface for making pastry on. One very simple way to make pastry successfully is to use a food processor, as the blade mixes the ingredients together quickly and effectively, though you should be careful not to overprocess it. Once you've made your pastry, it's very important to rest it in the refrigerator, as this allows the gluten to expand, enabling it to be rolled out. Having been rested and chilled, the pastry needs to be brought back to room temperature before you roll it out, otherwise it will crack.

Making granary bread

Extremely popular in Britain, granary bread uses a special brand of flour (obtainable from online suppliers), and is very simple to make. For extra fiber, the bread can be enriched by adding a teaspoon of fine wheat bran and then sprinkling it with a little more bran before baking. Its higher bran and wheatgerm content means that bread made with brown or wholewheat flour tends to have a denser texture than bread made with white flour.

2 teaspoons clear honey

1½ cups milk

2 x ¼-oz. packages dry yeast

5 cups granary flour (see page 000)

2 teaspoons salt, plus more
for glazing

I teaspoon bran, plus extra
for finishing

2 eggs

¾ stick unsalted butter, melted

**Makes 2 loaves
about 6½ x 4½ x 3 in.**

1 Put the honey with 5 tablespoons of the milk in a saucepan and heat it over a low heat until lukewarm. Remove from the heat, mix in the yeast thoroughly, then cover and leave to stand in a warm place for 15 minutes or until it bubbles. In a large bowl, sift in the flour (adding what gets left in the sieve) and salt. Add the bran, eggs, and melted butter and pour in the yeast mixture with the remaining milk. Using a wooden spoon, mix until the dough comes together.

2 Knead on a flat, lightly floured surface for about 10 minutes, or until the dough is smooth. Cover with a cloth and leave to rise in a warm place until it has doubled in size.

3 Preheat the oven to 450°F and lightly dust a baking tray with some flour. Knock back the dough by lifting it from the bowl and kneading it for a minute or so. Cut the dough in half and shape the pieces into two cigar-shaped loaves. Slash the tops with a knife. Place the loaves on the prepared baking tray, cover with a cloth, and leave to rise. When they have doubled in volume, they are ready to be baked.

4 Using a pastry brush, lightly brush the loaves with a salt glaze made by dissolving a pinch of salt in 2 tablespoons of hot water. Sprinkle the tops with more bran and bake in the preheated oven for about 20–30 minutes, or until brown. Remove from the tray and leave them to cool on the wire rack.

Making a sourdough starter

The aim here is to capture and grow natural yeasts—fungi—present in the air and on the flour. As they grow, they produce bubbles of carbon dioxide gas and lactic acid, which will eventually be used to leaven the dough and add flavor. For best results, use unbleached organic flour—white flour for a multipurpose starter, but rye or wholewheat flours can also be used. I recommend that you use spring water. If you use tap water, you should filter, boil, and cool it first. A kitchen work surface is usually the best place to raise a starter.

To begin

¾ cup unbleached organic white bread flour

½ cup tepid water (see recipe introduction above)

For each refreshment

¾ cup unbleached organic white bread flour

tepid water (see recipe introduction above)

1 Put the flour and water in a small bowl and mix to a thick, sticky paste. Cover the bowl with a damp dish towel or muslin secured with a rubber band—don't cover the bowl with plastic wrap. Leave it in a draft-free spot on a work surface, re-dampening the cloth as necessary.

2 After 2–4 days (depending on the conditions) the paste should have a skin and look bubbly. It should have a milky scent. If it smells bad, rather than slightly sour, or if you can see patches of mold, or if there are no signs of life, throw it away and start again. At this stage, you should give your starter its first feed, or refreshment. Add another ¾ cup flour and enough tepid water to make a soft, sticky pastelike dough. Work the dough with your hand or a wooden spoon to get plenty of air into the mixture. Cover the bowl again with a damp cloth and leave, as before, for 24 hours.

3 The starter should look very active now. Stir well, then remove and discard half of it. Add another ¾ cup flour and enough tepid water to make a dough as before. Cover and leave as before for 12 hours.

4 At this point, the sourdough starter should look very active and ready to use—to make sure there is enough to make a batch of bread and keep some for the next batch, you will need to increase the volume. You can do this by eye or by measuring—you will need about ¾ cup flour and enough water to make a soft, sticky dough as before. The dough should be bubbly again and ready to use after 6–8 hours. However, if the dough doesn't look active enough to use after its previous refreshment, you will need to halve it once more and feed it as before.

Note: Don't worry if your starter separates into a darkish liquid layer on top of a thicker paste. Just stir it up and feed as usual. This happens if you haven't fed the starter for a while, or if the starter is runny. If it smells strongly and makes your eyes water, it is in bad shape. Reduce it to a couple of tablespoons, then add flour and water in the same proportions as before every day until the starter is bubbly and has a milky aroma.

5 Once you have got a starter going, it will keep forever. If you look after it, you may never have to buy yeast or bread again. Feed it regularly, every 5 days or so, even if you are not using it (you can give away rather than discard half each time). Store it in a plastic container or glass jar in the refrigerator. When you want to use it, bring the starter back to room temperature, then feed it about 6 hours before starting the recipe. It should turn bubbly again.

Making California sourdough

There seem to be more recipes for California and San Francisco sourdough than there are bakers in the state. Before a loaf was shaped and baked, the original pioneers and settlers kept back a portion of dough to leaven the next batch. These days, bakers use a range of leavens; saved dough starter, soupy sourdough leavens, compressed yeast, dried sourdough flavorings, or baking soda. The objective is a light-textured, mildly sour, well-risen white loaf. The authentic flavor comes from the foggy atmosphere and the water of the Bay Area, which are hard to reproduce, but this is a good approximation.

1 cup sourdough starter (see page 54)

2 cups tepid water (see recipe introduction)

1 cake (0.6 oz.) compressed yeast (see note on p.57)

6½ cups unbleached white bread flour

2 teaspoons coarse sea salt

Makes 2 medium loaves

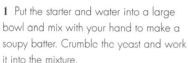

2 Mix the flour with the salt, then gradually beat it into the liquid with your hand until well mixed. The dough should feel soft but not sticky; if it feels too slack, work in extra flour, 1 tablespoon at a time; if it feels hard or dry, or there are crumbs left in the bottom of the bowl, work in extra water, 1 tablespoon at a time. Turn out onto a floured work surface and knead thoroughly to make a smooth, firm, very supple dough. Return the dough to the bowl and cover with plastic wrap. For the best flavor, let rise slowly in a cool room until doubled in size, about four hours, or overnight in the refrigerator.

1 Put the starter and water into a large bowl and mix with your hand to make a soupy batter. Crumble the yeast and work it into the mixture.

3 Turn out onto a lightly floured work surface and punch down to deflate. If the dough has been stored in the refrigerator, let it come back to room temperature for 1½–2 hours before continuing. Divide the dough into two equal pieces, cover with plastic wrap, and leave to rest for 10 minutes. Shape each portion into a neat ball, handling the dough as little as possible. Put onto two greased baking sheets, then slide into a large plastic bag, slightly inflate, and close the end. Leave to rise at normal room temperature until almost doubled in size, about 2 hours.

4 Meanwhile, preheat the oven to 425°F. Put a roasting pan of water into the oven to heat, as the steam created will help develop a good crust. Uncover the loaves and quickly slash the tops in a diamond pattern, using a serrated knife or a razor blade. Put into the heated, steamy oven and bake for 30 minutes or until the loaves sound hollow when tapped underneath. Cool on a wire rack and eat within five days, or toast. Can be frozen for up to a month.

Note: To use rapid-rising dry yeast, mix a half an envelope with the flour and salt, then work it into the sourdough starter and water mixture.

Making focaccia

A classic, olive oil-rich Italian bread that goes well with cold cured meats or antipasto, such as the vegetables sott'olio (page 118). Experiment by adding in different flavorings such as chopped olives, sun-dried tomatoes, or chopped herbs such as rosemary after the first rising stage.

3½ cups white bread flour

1 teaspoon sugar

1 teaspoon rapid-rising yeast

1 teaspoon fine salt

1¼ cups hand-hot water

6 tablespoons olive oil

2 teaspoons coarse salt crystals

Equipment needed
baking tile (optional) or baking sheet

Makes 1 loaf

1 Place the flour, sugar, yeast, and salt in a large mixing bowl and mix together. Pour in the hand-hot water and 3 tablespoons of the olive oil and gradually bring the mixture together to form a soft dough.

2 Transfer the dough onto a lightly floured surface and knead it for around 10 minutes until it feels smooth and supple. Cover the dough with a clean, damp dish towel and set aside in a warm place for 1 hour until the dough has risen and is roughly doubled in size. Break down the risen dough by kneading briefly. Place on an oiled baking sheet and press out the dough into a large oval about ½ in. thick. Cover with a clean dish towel and set side for another 30 minutes.

3 Preheat the oven to 475°F. Preheat the baking tile if you are using one, or the baking sheet. Use your fingertips to press down into the dough, dimpling its surface.

4 Pour the remaining olive oil on top, spreading it evenly over the surface of the dough. Sprinkle the coarse salt crystals on top. Place the focaccia on the preheated baking tile or baking sheet. Bake in the oven for 15–20 minutes until golden brown. Remove from the oven and cool on a wire rack. Serve either warm or at room temperature.

Making sweet piecrust

This rich, sweet piecrust, a staple of pâtissiers, is ideal for sweet pies and tarts. It can be made in advance, wrapped well, and frozen for up to a year, to use as required. This recipe is ample for a 10—11-in. single crust pie; for a double crust pie, simply double the quantities given (you may have some left over for a tartlet or two).

1½ cups (rounded) white all-purpose flour

pinch of salt

1 teaspoon superfine sugar

1 stick butter, diced

1 egg yolk

3-4 tablespoons cold water

Makes enough piecrust to line a 10-in. pie pan or flan tin

1 If making by hand, sift the flour and salt into a mixing bowl. Mix in the sugar.

2 Add the diced butter to the bowl and, working quickly and using your fingertips, rub the butter into the flour until absorbed.

3 Make a well in the center of the mixture and place the egg yolk in the well.

4 Add 3 tablespoons of the water and mix together quickly and thoroughly with a knife until the mixture forms into a soft, sticky dough. Add some or all of the remaining water if necessary.

5 If using a food processor, place the flour, salt, and sugar in the food processor and blend briefly to mix. Add the diced butter and blend thoroughly.

6 Add the egg yolk and 2 tablespoons of cold water, mix lightly with a knife, and blend until the mixture comes together to form a soft dough, adding another tablespoon of cold water if necessary.

7 Once you've made the dough, either by hand or in the food processor, transfer it to a lightly floured surface and knead gently until the pastry becomes smooth and pliable. Wrap in plastic wrap and chill in the refrigerator for 30 minutes to rest the pastry before using it.

Using your produce

Wild mushroom and garlic pizza

Bread flour is higher in gluten than all-purpose flour, and this will give your home-made pizza dough a lovely elastic texture.

For the dough

1¼ cups warm water

1½ teaspoons active dry yeast

pinch of sugar

3¼ cups white bread flour, plus extra for dusting

1 teaspoon salt

2 tablespoons olive oil

For the topping

1 stick butter

1 lb. 2 oz. wild mushrooms, wiped clean, trimmed, and thinly sliced

3 garlic cloves, peeled and minced

coarse sea salt and freshly ground black pepper

1 mozzarella ball, approx. 5 oz., thinly sliced

4 sprigs of fresh thyme

Makes 4 x 10-in. pizzas

1 To make the dough, pour the water into a measuring pitcher, add the yeast and sugar, and leave for 5–10 minutes in a warm place until frothy. Sift the flour and salt into a large mixing bowl, then stir in the frothy yeast mixture and the olive oil.

2 Mix well together, then tip the dough out onto a floured work surface. Knead for about 5 minutes until the dough is silky and elastic. Dust with a little flour, put into a bowl, cover, and leave in a warm place for about 1 hour until the dough has doubled in size. Knock back the risen dough with your knuckles and divide into four pieces. Roll out each with a rolling pin and, using your fingers, stretch to a 9–10-in. round.

3 Preheat the oven to 400°F. Place a lightly oiled baking sheet in the oven to heat up. Melt the butter in a large skillet, add the mushrooms, and sauté gently for about 2–3 minutes until thoroughly coated in butter. Stir in the garlic and seasoning and remove from the heat.

4 Brush the pizza bases with garlic butter taken from the mushroom pan. Scatter with the mozzarella and top with the mushrooms and sprigs of thyme. Brush with the remaining butter from the pan and bake in the preheated oven for 10–15 minutes or until the cheese has melted. Scatter with coarsely ground black pepper and serve.

Variations:

Potato and rosemary pizza

Replace the mushrooms with 3 large parboiled, thinly sliced potatoes and the thyme with 2 sprigs of rosemary, minced.

Asparagus, bacon, and egg pizza

Replace the mushrooms with 1 lb. asparagus spears. Replace the thyme with 3 strips of thick Canadian bacon, roughly chopped. Add 1 medium egg cracked over the asparagus and bacon about 2 minutes before the end of cooking.

Wild arugula and dry-cured ham

Replace the mushrooms with 1 bunch of trimmed whole green onions. Replace the thyme with 4 thin slices of dry-cured ham, such as prosciutto, and add 7 cups wild arugula leaves on top.

Traditional tomato and garlic bruschetta

This is bruschetta at its simplest and best. Use only the best and freshest ingredients for this recipe, and for authenticity, you should use only the finest Tuscan extra-virgin olive oil. The ripe tomato is just crushed in your hand and smashed onto the fresh bread, then eaten immediately.

4 large, very ripe tomatoes

coarse sea salt and freshly ground black pepper

4 thick slices of sourdough bread (see page 56)

2 garlic cloves, halved

extra-virgin olive oil, for drizzling

Serves 4

1 Roughly chop the tomatoes and season with salt and pepper.

2 To make the bruschetta, broil, toast, or pan-grill the bread on both sides until lightly charred or toasted. Rub the top side of each slice with the cut garlic, then drizzle with olive oil.

3 Spoon the tomatoes over the bruschetta and drizzle with more olive oil. Eat immediately with your fingers!

Chicken in a loaf

The idea for this recipe comes from southern Italy, where it is served cut in thick slices.

5 tablespoons extra-virgin olive oil

3-lb. chicken, cut into pieces

2 cups chicken stock

1 loaf of granary bread (see page 52), baked as a round

¼ cup shelled almonds, toasted

¼ cup shelled pistachios

2 eggs

juice of 1 lemon

⅜ (scant) cup capers, drained

bunch of flat-leaf parsley, chopped

salt and freshly ground black pepper

Equipment needed

food processor

Serves 6–8

1 Using a heavy-based pan that has a tight-fitting lid, heat 3 tablespoons of the oil over medium heat and brown the chicken pieces all over. Pour in 1 cup of the stock and cook until the chicken is tender, adding more stock if the pan looks in danger of drying out. Drain the chicken and leave it to cool, reserving the stock.

2 Preheat the oven to 350°F. Prepare the bread "dish" and "lid" by cutting the loaf in two horizontally, about one-third down from the top. Hollow it out carefully so as not to tear the crust, keeping the soft dough from the center. Brush the crust all over, both inside and out, with the remaining olive oil.

3 Put both the almonds and pistachios in a food processor, along with the dough from inside the loaf, and blitz until reduced to the texture of fine crumbs. With the machine still running, slowly add the rest of the stock, the eggs and lemon juice. Add a little extra stock, if needed, for a runny consistency.

4 When the chicken is cool enough to handle, skin it and remove the flesh from the bones. Cut the meat into small pieces and stir in the capers and parsley, followed by the sauce. Season and spoon the mixture into the prepared bread crust. Cover with the lid and bake in the oven for 20 minutes or until golden. Serve hot or cold.

Leaf salad with vinaigrette and croutons

Croutons add a deliciously crisp contrast in texture to a salad and can be made from any bread, including leftover, stale slices. These croutons would also be delicious in a soup.

2 small Boston lettuces, washed and torn

1 lollo rosso lettuce, washed and torn

½ curly endive, washed and torn

good handful of purslane, washed and torn

pinch of coarse sea salt

For the croutons

2 thick slices of granary bread, crusts removed (see page 52)

1 garlic clove, peeled

1 tablespoon olive oil

1 tablespoon butter

For the creamy vinaigrette

1 tablespoon light cream

2 teaspoons sherry vinegar

5 tablespoons olive oil

freshly ground black pepper

Serves 4

1 Place all the leaves in a large salad bowl, mix together, and scatter the salt on top.

2 Meanwhile, to make the croutons, cut the slices of bread into small cubes. Rub the inside of a skillet with the garlic clove, heat the olive oil together with the butter in the pan, and fry the bread cubes for 4–5 minutes, turning them over until evenly crisp and golden. Drain on paper towels.

3 To make the dressing, combine the cream with the sherry vinegar and beat in the olive oil. Pour over the salad leaves, toss together well, and finish with freshly ground pepper. Scatter the croutons on top of the dressed salad.

Apple betty with dried cranberries

This is a traditional American recipe with very humble origins. It is always made with apples, but not necessarily dried cranberries. It is an economical way to use up stale bread, but it tastes even better if you use fresh white bread or even brioche.

2 lb. tart eating apples, such as Granny Smith, peeled, cored, and diced

1 teaspoon ground cinnamon

1 tablespoon finely grated orange zest

⅜ cup fresh apple or orange juice

¾ cup dried cranberries

6 cups breadcrumbs (see page 52)

¾ stick unsalted butter, melted

¾ cup chopped shelled pecans

⅜ (rounded) cup light soft brown sugar

2 tablespoons unsalted butter, cut into pieces

whipped cream, to serve

Serves 4–6

1 Preheat the oven to 375°F.

2 Combine the apples, cinnamon, orange zest, apple juice, and cranberries in a large bowl. Toss gently with your hands to mix and set aside.

3 In a separate bowl, combine the breadcrumbs and melted butter and mix well. Spread about one-third of the buttered breadcrumbs in the bottom of a well-buttered baking dish. Add the pecans and sugar to the remaining crumbs and mix to combine.

4 Put half of the apple mixture on top of the breadcrumbs in the baking dish. Top with half the breadcrumb and pecan mixture and top this with the remaining apple mixture. Finish with the remainder of the breadcrumb and pecan mixture. Dot with the butter and bake in the preheated oven for 30–40 minutes, until golden and crisp. Serve warm with whipped cream.

Apple tart

Apple tart is a classic use for sweet piecrust, but this recipe represents a slight departure. The combination of apples and vanilla is divine, so I have added a layer of vanilla-scented apple purée. Serve warm or at room temperature with whipped cream or vanilla ice cream.

1 batch sweet piecrust, chilled and rested (see page 60)

3 sweet eating apples, such as Golden Delicious, peeled, cored, and sliced

1 tablespoon unsalted butter, melted

1 tablespoon sugar

whipped cream or vanilla ice cream, to serve

For the apple and vanilla purée

3 apples (any variety), peeled, cored, and diced

1 vanilla bean, split lengthwise

2–4 tablespoons sugar (depends on sweetness of apples)

2 teaspoons unsalted butter

Equipment needed

food processor

blender or food mill

11-in. shallow, loose-base tart pan

Serves 6–8

1 Preheat the oven to 375°F and generously butter the tart pan.

2 Roll out the rested piecrust into a circle about ¼ in. thick and slightly larger than the pan. Line the pan with it, trim the edges, prick the bottom with a fork, and cover with waxed paper weighted down with some baking beans. Bake blind in the preheated oven for 15 minutes. Remove from the oven and leave to cool slightly.

3 To make the apple purée, put the diced apples, vanilla, sugar, and butter in a saucepan with 3–4 tablespoons water.

Cook gently for about 10–15 minutes, stirring often until soft and adding more water if necessary. Use the tip of a small knife to scrape the seeds out of the vanilla bean, then discard the bean.

4 Transfer the mixture to a food processor, blender, or food mill and purée until smooth.

5 Spread the purée evenly in the pie shell. Carefully arrange the apple slices in a neat circle around the edge; they should be slightly overlapping but not completely squashed together. Repeat to create an inner circle, trimming the slices slightly so that they fit, going in the opposite direction from the outer circle. Brush with melted butter and sprinkle the sugar on top.

6 Bake in the oven until just browned and tender, 25–35 minutes. Serve warm or at room temperature with whipped cream or vanilla ice cream.

Rhubarb and marmalade tart

Rhubarb tends to collapse into a mush when cooked and can spoil the piecrust in a tart. To prevent this, dry-fry it first in sugar for just long enough to let its juices start to run but keeping it firm enough to stand the pieces upright in the tart.

1 tablespoon unsalted butter, plus extra for greasing

1 batch sweet piecrust, chilled and rested (see page 60)

1 lb. rhubarb

2 tablespoons superfine sugar

4 tablespoons coarse marmalade

1 tablespoon whiskey

Equipment needed

8-in. loose-base tart pan or 4 individual tart pans

Serves 4–6

1 Preheat the oven to 375°F and generously butter the tart pan or individual tart pans.

2 Roll out the rested piecrust into a circle about ¼ in. thick and slightly larger than the pan. Line the pan(s) with it, trim the edges, prick the bottom(s) with a fork, and cover with waxed paper weighted down with some baking beans. Bake blind in the preheated oven for 15 minutes. Remove from the oven and leave to cool slightly. Turn up the oven to 450°F.

3 Meanwhile, cut the rhubarb into 2-in. lengths. Put them into a saucepan with the sugar and cook gently over low heat for about 5–7 minutes, shaking the pan occasionally, until the rhubarb releases some of its juices but is still firm enough to handle. Strain, reserving the juices, and leave to cool.

4 When the pastry is slightly cooled, use a pastry brush to paint the base(s) and sides with 2 tablespoons of the marmalade. Stand the pieces of rhubarb upright in the tart pan(s), packing them in tightly, dot the top(s) with the butter, cover with waxed paper, and bake in the preheated oven for about 15 minutes. Remove from the oven and leave to cool slightly.

5 To make the glaze: in a saucepan boil the rhubarb juices over high heat to reduce to about 1 teaspoon. Stir in the remaining marmalade and the whiskey and, stirring constantly, continue boiling to reduce by about half. Using a pastry brush, paint the glaze over the top of the fruit. Allow to cool before serving.

Chapter 3

THE CANDY STORE

Born with what seems to be a natural sweet tooth, people have long prized sweet foods. The result of this long-standing fascination with sweetness is a rich and diverse world of confectionery. For many centuries, candies and other sweets were luxuries, made for and enjoyed by a wealthy elite, with the creating of confectionery a special skill, characterized by creativity and inventiveness. Candy may be more commonplace these days, but those made with the finest ingredients and lots of care and attention will always stand out from the others.

Sugar and chocolate are at the heart of Western confectionery today, but the earliest known sweetener was honey, and human beings have been harvesting it from the hives of wild bees for at least 10,000 years. Although honey is always sweet, its flavor depends on the flowers from which the bees have gathered the nectar, because the flowers add their own aromatic qualities to the honey. Monofloral honeys—that is, honeys produced from the nectar of one type of plant—range enormously in taste and color, from the mild sweetness of a clover honey to the almost bitter tang of chestnut honey. The ancient Egyptians valued honey highly, and archaeological evidence shows that by around 2,600 B.C.E., the Egyptians had developed beekeeping.

Sugar, however, was to replace honey in its role as a prized sweetener. Sugar cane, a tall grass with a sweet-tasting juice, has a long history of cultivation in Asia. The first reference to solid sugar, made by boiling down the sugar cane juice until it crystallized, is on a Persian tablet of 510 B.C.E. The knowledge of, and taste for, sugar spread from the Middle East to Western Europe, where sugar was to be a luxury product until the eighteenth century. In contrast to its sweet, pleasurable image, however, is the stark reality that the market for sugar fueled the slave trade, with Africans transported in huge numbers to the Americas to work on sugarcane plantations. Other sources of sweetness include sweet saps, such as North America's maple syrup, which is made from the sap of the maple tree, and Scandinavia's birch syrup. The nineteenth century saw the discovery that sugar could also be derived from a European vegetable—the sugar beet. Today, sugar from both beet and cane is cheap and widely available, and candies made from sugar are for many an everyday treat rather than a luxury.

Nowadays, we take it for granted that chocolate is a key ingredient in confectionery, but for much of its history

chocolate was consumed as a beverage, rather than in the solid form with which we are so familiar today. Chocolate is derived from the bitter-tasting beans of the cacao tree (*Theobroma cacao*), which is indigenous to Latin America. There are several varieties of cacao tree, with three main groups cultivated for use in the chocolate industry: Criollo, Forastero, and Trinitario. Criollo, low yielding and susceptible to disease, produces the rarest and most highly prized cacao beans, noted for their delicate flavor. In contrast, Forastero is a robust, high-yielding variety with a slightly bitter flavor, which provides the bulk of the world's cacao. A hybrid of Criollo and Forastero, Trinitario is more flavorful than Forastero and more resistant to disease than Criollo. Both the Mayan and Aztec civilizations valued cacao, using it to make a drink. The Spanish explorers who conquered Central America in the sixteenth century brought the cacao bean back to Europe. There, they too ground the beans to make a drink, called chocolate, which was prized as an expensive novelty.

Technological advances during the eighteenth and nineteenth centuries resulted in the making of eating chocolate. A key stage was the invention by Dutchman, Conrad van Houten, of a screw press, patented in 1828, which separated cocoa butter (the fat found naturally in cacao beans) from the paste, leaving behind cocoa powder. Following this came the discovery that cocoa butter could be mixed with ground cacao beans to make a smooth paste that was solid when cool, but melted in the mouth—in short, eating chocolate.

Understanding how to work with sugar and chocolate is the key to producing your own candies and chocolates successfully at home. As with baking, the art of confectionery requires precision and an eye for the details of the process.

Above far left: Sugar cooked to the soft ball stage
Above center left: Shavings of chocolate used for decoration
Above center right: Raw cocoa beans
Above right: The finest chocolate has a cocoa content of at least 70%

Sugar

Sugar has long been valued for its sweet flavor. In addition to its taste, however, sugar has other remarkable properties that make it, when heated, an extraordinarily versatile ingredient. When heated with water, sugar melts into a syrup. Heating this syrup to different degrees produces confectionery with a range of diverse textures, from soft, yielding fudge or taffy to hard lollipops and brittle praline.

There are many different types of sugar to choose from, with differences arising from the degree of refining and the size of sugar crystal created. When sugar is extracted from the juice of sugar cane or beet, it leaves behind a residue: a sticky black syrup called molasses. White sugar is made by removing the molasses entirely, while brown sugars retain varying amounts of molasses, ranging in color from golden to dark brown. The more molasses a sugar contains, the darker the color, the stickier the crystals, and the stronger the flavor; for example, dark brown soft sugar has a more pronounced taste than light brown soft sugar. When it comes to making confectionery, fully refined white sugars, which have no flavor other than sweetness, are both neutral and extremely versatile. White granulated sugar, for example, can be used to make candies such as butterscotch. White sugar, rather than brown, is also the easiest to caramelize, since you can

judge the different stages by the color the sugar turns to as it moves from pale gold to dark brown. Brown sugars, with their more pronounced taste, are often used to give extra flavor to non-chocolate candy confectionery, such as caramels. Sugar candies are also given an extra taste dimension by the addition of flavorings, such as peppermint, coffee, or citrus fruits.

In addition to varying heat levels, confectioners use a number of different techniques, such as physically manipulating the syrup, to produce the required texture and flavor from sugar syrups. The deliberate introduction of what are called 'interfering agents', such as liquid glucose or lemon juice, to inhibit crystallization is another way in which different textures are created. Working rapidly at the "soft crack" stage (see page 86), sugar syrup is pulled and stretched to create opaque, open-textured humbugs, whilst "hard crack" syrup is twisted into traditional barley sugar twists. Simply stirring the syrup at various stages is another way of affecting the resulting end texture.

Caramels and toffees

Caramels and toffees can be made in a number of ways, with the syrup cooked to the "soft ball" stage at a temperature of 234–240°F for caramels and soft toffees or to the "hard ball" stage, that is a temperature of 250–266°F, for hard toffees. It is often enriched with the addition of dairy ingredients, such as butter or cream, and may be flavored with ingredients such as corn syrup or rum. Usually the toffee syrup is simply poured out into a baking pan or onto a slab and left to cool, marked into squares when just hardened, then broken into pieces.

Toffee is one of the most popular candies in Britain. Established in 1910, The Toffee Shop, in England's Lake District, has long been noted for the quality of its fudge and toffee, which are made on the premises in a kitchen at the back of the shop.

"The way we make our fudge and toffee and the ingredients we use are the same as it's always been made here," explains owner Neil Boustead, who works in the shop, together with seven staff. "The recipes have been handed down from the first owner, Mrs Furnass. Nothing has changed. It's made by hand, stirred by hand, wrapped by hand.

"We make our fudge from sugar, butter, milk, and partially inverted syrup. We make it in small batches using 12 old-fashioned jam pans and keep a very close eye on it as it cooks to make sure it doesn't catch [stick]. Getting the temperature right is vital; we use thermometers for that. What makes the difference is that we beat our fudge by hand, which gives it its texture. We have to be careful as the fudge can be overbeaten or underbeaten. That wouldn't affect the taste, but it would affect the texture. I can tell when I cut the fudge whether it's right or not. A lot of people think of fudge as very soft. Ours is more like Scottish tablet, which is hard and crystally. Our fudge isn't Scottish tablet, but does have a crumbly texture."

In addition to their famous fudge—butter, chocolate, and mint-flavored—The Toffee Shop does produce toffee: butter and treacle. "There's no milk in our toffee," says Mr. Boustead; "we use vinegar. It's very time-consuming to produce the toffee because it's broken by hand and wrapped by hand. A half-pound block of fudge can be cut and wrapped by me in a minute. The same weight of toffee would take much longer. Every piece is a different shape and each piece is individually wrapped. You can taste the butter in our butter toffee, and our treacle toffee has a real treacle taste. Some people make all sorts of flavors. We stick to just five classic flavors with our fudge and toffee."

Fudge

Long before it acquired its chocolate guise, fudge was flavored mainly with sugar. In order to make basic fudge, the sugar syrup is traditionally enriched by adding butter, cream, or milk. This syrup is then cooked until it reaches the "soft ball" stage (see page 86), at a temperature of 234–240°F. How the fudge is treated at this stage will affect its texture. For a firm-textured, granular fudge, the mixture is beaten vigorously while still hot. Allowing the fudge mixture to cool and crystallize first before beating it results in fudge with a smoother texture.

Right and left: An assortment of vanilla, cherry and walnut, and chocolate fudge

Marshmallows and nougat

Marshmallows are made by boiling sugar syrup until it reaches the "hard ball" stage—that is, a temperature of 250–266°F (see page 86). The syrup is then combined with other ingredients, such as gelatin, whisked egg whites or light cornsyrup, and whisked until light—a process that incorporates air into the mixture and gives marshmallows their characteristic fluffy texture. Nougat is made similarly, though often with the addition of nuts, with the nougat mixture spread out in an even layer and weighted down to compress it, so producing a denser, chewier texture than that of marshmallows.

Lollipops

Hard sugar-based candy, such as lollipops, is produced by taking syrup to the high temperature of 300°F, with different flavorings and colorings added to the base syrup as desired.

Praline and nut brittles

Caramelization is achieved at the highest temperatures on the sugar stages chart (see page 86) of 320–351°F. As the sugar caramelizes, it creates distinctive flavors, the sugar becoming darker in appearance and more bitter in flavor the longer it is caramelized. Praline and nut brittles are produced using caramelization.

Crystallized flowers

Crystallized flowers, traditionally rose petals and violets, are produced in less time-consuming ways. One way is to coat them with a sugar syrup, stirring them until the sugar recrystallizes. Another is to brush the flowers or petals with egg white or a solution of a natural resin called gum arabic, then sprinkle them with superfine sugar and set them aside to dry.

Above left: Marshmallows dusted with confectioners' sugar and cornflour
Above right: Lollipops made with button-shaped molds
Right: An assortment of candied fruits

Candied fruits and nuts

Sugar syrups are also key to candied fruits and nuts—a historic way of both preserving fruits and nuts and transforming them into luxurious treats that have been enjoyed for centuries. This is a time-consuming process, which takes place over days. The first stage sees firm-textured fruits, such as citrus fruits, stone fruits such as plums or apricots, or slices of pineapple, poached in order to help them absorb the syrup, then immersed in a strong sugar syrup and left for 24 hours. Each following day, the fruit are removed from the syrup, which is then further sweetened and concentrated before the fruit are immersed in it again, then finally set aside to dry out. This gradual process allows the fruit or nut to become saturated with the syrup while preserving a soft texture. A final coating in superfine sugar creates crystallized fruit, while dipping candied fruit in syrup creates smooth coated glacé fruit.

Meet the producer: Sweet Treats

Run by Nia Wood and Mike Watt, this boutique confectionery company specializes in a range of pretty, handmade candies, produced by Nia and Mike in their small kitchen in a converted barn.

"We're particularly known for our handmade marshmallows," explains Nia. "They were the first sweet that I made commercially and they're quite unusual, not something you find everywhere. They're very different from factory-made ones; much softer, they melt in your mouth. Grownups love them just as much as children. I make them in different flavors. Lemon meringue and raspberry are the stand-out flavors. I'm always experimenting, but I only want to use natural ingredients, so I squeeze the lemon juice and use fresh raspberries. My marshmallows don't keep well, because they're made with fresh ingredients. They have a shelf life of just six weeks. I make them in small batches to keep them fresh; I don't have a huge back-stock.

"Working in confectionery, you've got to be exact with your ratios and measurements; it's very precise. I've always liked baking and making desserts. The secret to making the marshmallows is to get the sugar syrup right. It's very important to dissolve all the sugar before it comes to the boil. Then it's very tempting to stir the syrup when it's boiling, but you mustn't, as it will re-crystallize. You have to keep your eye on the syrup, as it will suddenly get very hot, very fast."

In addition to marshmallows, Nia makes a range of other candies, including caramels. "When I cook them I do it by eye, by color, by smell. I'm experimenting with different sugars in my caramels. I want to get a real depth of flavor. I'm also working on making *pâtes de fruits*; it takes a lot of fruit purée to make them. I am a perfectionist, so it takes time before I introduce a new line. I've got to be really happy before I sell it."

Chocolate

The chocolate available to the domestic cook has already undergone a complex process of transformation, from the starting point of the raw cacao bean to the dark, smooth substance we know as chocolate. Unlike sugar, which had a long history of use before mechanization, chocolate acquired its form as something to be eaten only comparatively recently, along with developments in manufacturing processes.

The process by which raw cacao beans are transformed into eating chocolate is a lengthy one. First, the beans are fermented; then roasted to develop color and flavor; then ground into a liquid paste called cacao liquor or cacao mass. The cacao liquor can be processed further to extract the cocoa butter and create cocoa powder. Dark chocolate is created by mixing cacao liquor, sugar, and cocoa butter into a paste. In the United States an unsweetened form of dark chocolate is often used for baking. Milk solids can be added to create

milk chocolate. This mixture is first refined by being passed through rollers, then conched (stirred mechanically for a few hours to a few days to homogenize the chocolate and bring out the flavors), returning the chocolate to liquid form. The chocolate is tempered by being passed through a precise process of repeated heating and cooling, to stabilize the cocoa fat. Then it can be molded into shapes such as bars.

The higher the cocoa content in chocolate, the less sugar it will contain and the more bitter the chocolate will taste, with 100% chocolate being very bitter indeed, as it contains no sugar whatsoever. Milk chocolate contains cacao liquor, cocoa butter, sugar, and milk solids. Its lower cocoa butter content makes it usually softer in texture than dark chocolate.

Use good-quality chocolate with a high cocoa content (60–70%) for making chocolates at home. Experiment with brands and cocoa contents. Chocolate made by reputable producers will have a better flavor and texture than cheap chocolate because the latter is often made with cheaper and softer vegetable fats instead of costly cocoa butter.

Working with chocolate at home usually involves returning it to a liquid state by melting it. Professional chocolatiers temper their chocolate before working with it. When done correctly, this slow process of heating and cooling produces glossy chocolate with a pleasing brittle snap when broken and a good shelf life. The melted chocolate can then be poured into molds and allowed to set, creating simple chocolate bars and hollow shapes, as well as dainty cases to be filled with a sweet flavoring and topped with a layer of chocolate.

Left: Studies have shown that consuming small amounts of dark chocolate regularly can benefit the body's circulatory system

Meet the producer: Paul A. Young

Fizzing with energy and enthusiasm for his craft, Paul A. Young opts for a purist, labor-intensive approach to his chocolate making.

"Everything we do is handmade. For me, that's what being an artisan is about. Anyone can order pre-made fillings, pre-made shells, and use a tempering machine. We temper on a marble slab; we don't have a tempering machine," he explains. "Tempering is the trickiest part to get right. You have to get it to the right degree; if not, you get bloomed chocolate, chocolate that's not shiny, cracked chocolate. I guess I'm very old-fashioned, but I don't trust thermometers. We know our chocolate is right by touch and feel, by sight. Each chocolate has its own character and texture. It takes a long time to gain this knowledge." The advantage of this insistence on traditional crafts and the acquisition of skills is that Paul can achieve exactly the results he wants. "The advantage of marble tempering is that I can balance the chocolate, adjust the flavoring."

Fine ingredients are at the core of Paul's luxurious chocolate range. "We buy the best chocolate we can, not cheap sugary stuff, and are as seasonal as possible when it comes to ingredients. Unrefined organic sugar —I don't like anything that's over-processed. I use a French butter that I've used all my pâtisserie career, which is very smooth and not over-heavy, and our eggs are always free-range. Our ganache only lasts seven days; we make it every day, working like a pâtisserie."

Paul is known for his daring flavors, such as Port and Stilton. "My flavors are very distinct; you know what you're eating. I always try to be true to the flavors. For example, our champagne truffle is just champagne and chocolate, no cream, no butter. I like a champagne that's not too dry and match it with a very smooth chocolate. I don't want my chocolates to taste generic; you can get that processed, sugar-heavy taste. Everything should taste individual." Inspired by the power of sweets and to be evocative, Paul's new direction is distinctly creative. "My new signature chocolate is called Burning Embers," he declares. "It looks like a little bit of coal and I've flavored it with chili, cedar wood, and pine, to make you think of sitting in front of a fire on a winter evening."

Liquid chocolate is highly valued as a dipping medium, used to coat an assortment of fillings. The range of possible fillings is huge: shelled nuts, candied fruits such as orange peel, raisins, marzipan, chocolate truffles, and flavored fondant creams such as peppermint or orange are all classic fillings. A liquid liqueur, inside a sugar crystal shell, is another traditional filling. As an elegant finishing touch, the chocolate casing can be decorated in a number of ways, including using a confectioner's dipping fork to add textured patterns while the coating is still soft, finely piping on chocolate patterns, or sprinkling on a decorative garnish. The use of edible stencils to add a colored pattern to the surface of a square chocolate has become increasingly popular among professional chocolatiers.

Chocolate is also used to create ganache, classically made from a mixture of melted chocolate and scalded cream, sometimes with the addition of butter. Ganache is used both to make truffles and as a filling for truffles. The chosen ratio of chocolate to cream affects the texture of the ganache, with a higher chocolate content producing a firmer ganache with a richer chocolate flavor. There are different ways of making the ganache filling. The chocolate can be melted first, then mixed with the warm cream, or finely chopped, then melted by adding warm cream. The texture of the ganache can then be lightened by whisking. The ganache can be flavored in many different ways, classically by adding a small amount of alcohol, such as rum, brandy, or Champagne, direct to the ganache.

Meet the producer: William Curley

Known for his elegant and accomplished creations, chocolatier and pâtissier William Curley gained his expertise working as a pâtissier in Michelin-starred restaurants with top chefs including Pierre Koffman, Raymond Blanc, and Marco Pierre White.

"Working with pastry, chocolate plays a large part in what you do, so you learn skills such as tempering," he explains. "When it came to setting up my own business, this background, where you don't compromise on the product or the ingredients, has really influenced me. I use the best ingredients in my chocolates and pastries: Amedei, which, in my opinion, is the finest couverture, good-quality cream, really good butter. There's a subtlety to my chocolates, and because we're using Amedei [brand], we always want to be able to taste the chocolate, rather than overpower it with the flavorings." There's also a characteristic intricacy to William's chocolates: Piedmont hazelnut contains a layer of crushed hazelnuts mixed with feuilletine crumbs, praline, and chocolate, set, then topped with a gianduja ganache.

William works with his Japanese wife, Suzue, also an acclaimed pâtissier, and there is a distinctive Japanese element to the flavorings. "It just came about naturally," he explains. "I started with classic flavors, but began to push the boundaries a bit, using fresh herbs like mint, rosemary, and lemon thyme. On a trip to Japan, I spent a lot of time looking at ingredients there and brought some back and started experimenting with them: ingredients like Japanese black vinegar, sesame, yuzu. I wanted to be original, but not to shock for shock's sake. Probably our most surprising chocolate is my apricot and wasabi—a layer of apricot paste with wasabi ganache on top. You get the apricot first, fruity and slightly sharp, then the wasabi hit at the end, but not too much; you wouldn't want it to be too powerful."

Sourcing the ingredients

Chocolate

As already mentioned, cocoa beans undergo an intricate and complex process in becoming eating chocolate. This processed chocolate, in turn, can be used as the starting point for making your own chocolate creations. It's worth realizing that even the most experienced chocolatiers work with chocolate that has already been refined, with major chocolate producers offering a range of high-quality chocolates that are the starting point for making chocolate candy. One guideline for judging the quality of the chocolate you are buying is to look at the cocoa content; reputable brands declare the level of cocoa content on the label. When choosing dark chocolate, many chocolatiers recommend looking for around 65–73% cocoa content. Bear in mind that milk chocolate, made by the addition of milk solids, has by its nature a lower cocoa content than dark. Read the label to check that cocoa butter, rather than vegetable fat, has been used, as another indication of good quality.

Remember that different cocoa contents will produce varying results; a recipe that works with a high-cocoa-content dark chocolate may not work as well if you substitute a low-cocoa content milk chocolate. Professional chocolatiers and pâtissiers use couverture chocolate, a chocolate with a high cocoa butter content, specially made for use as a coating chocolate, which requires tempering before use.

Sugar

"Unrefined" sugars, such as brown crystal sugar, retain a natural color and flavor that more processed refined sugars lack. Look for the word "unrefined" when choosing brown sugars, as inferior brown sugars are made by simply adding coloring to refined white sugar and lack the depth of flavor that true brown sugars have.

Match the sugar to what you are making. White sugar has a neutral sweetness that makes it a very versatile and widely used sugar in cooking. For a more distinctive flavor, look to unrefined sugars.

White refined granulated sugar A sugar that has medium-size crystals, measuring 0.3–0.5mm.

Superfine sugar Also called fine granulated sugar, this has small crystals, around 0.1–0.3mm, which dissolve much more quickly than ordinary granulated sugar.

Brown crystal sugar A raw cane sugar, originally from Demerara in Guyana, this sparkling golden sugar has large crunchy crystals and is used to add texture as well as sweetness.

Preserving sugar Specially created for use in preserving, this sugar has large crystals (1–2mm in size), which dissolve very fast when heated, so cutting down on the risk of caramelization and burning.

Confectioners' sugar This extremely fine sugar, with its powdered crystals measuring 0.01–0.1mm, requires only moisture, rather than heat, to dissolve it. It is typically used to make frosting.

Muscovado sugar Also called Barbados sugar, this fine-grained sugar is dark brown and has a sticky texture and rich, full flavor.

How to store

Sugar should be stored in a cool, dark, dry place, where it is free from any risk of moisture getting in.

Chocolate should be stored in a cool, dark, dry place, such as a kitchen cabinet, where it will keep well, ideally in an airtight container. Dark chocolate has the best keeping qualities, while white chocolate (made from cocoa butter and sugar, but no cacao liquor) is the most perishable.

Opposite: Examples of William Curley's elegant chocolate creations

Techniques

You will often find yourself working with both sugar and chocolate when making confectionary, as these two ingredients are the starting point for creating numerous recipes. They each require very different handling and the few golden rules outlined below as to how to cook with them are a useful starting point for successful sweet-making.

Recommended equipment for making confectionery:
accurate scales
candy thermometer
double boiler
cool surface for working on, such as a marble board
long-handled confectioners' dipping fork

Cooking with sugar

A sugar syrup is the starting point for many confectionery items, from the soft fondant centers found in candies such as peppermint creams to gaudy, glossy lollipops. To make your sugar syrup successfully, first dissolve the sugar thoroughly in the water, stirring it as it dissolves. Once the syrup is boiling, however, DO NOT STIR IT until it reaches the desired temperature, as this causes crystallization and interferes with the cooking process.

As the sugar syrup cooks, it reaches a range of stages that produce different results (see page 86). Investing in a sugar or jam thermometer to measure the temperature of your sugar syrup is a simple way to ensure that you know when you've reached the correct stage. Alternatively, you can test the temperature of the syrup by carefully checking how a small portion of the syrup behaves when cooled in water, a test called the "cold water test" and a method used by confectioners for hundreds of years. The texture of the syrup, ranging from "thread" to "hard crack," tells you what stage you are at.

A sugar syrup is made from a mixture of water and sugar, with the water then cooked off during the syrup making. The reason that water is added to the sugar is that sugar burns very easily when heated, so adding the water reduces the risk of burning. It also allows the sugar to be cooked for longer, so developing more flavor. As the water content is cooked off, the sugar heating process accelerates, becoming hotter and hotter, faster and faster, so you need to keep an eagle eye on proceedings at the later stages. Bear in mind that working with sugar syrups requires care, as these syrups become EXTREMELY hot.

Cooking with chocolate

Working with chocolate often involves melting it into a liquid state. The key to melting chocolate successfully is that this should be a very gentle process, because if chocolate gets too hot, it separates. It's worth remembering that milk chocolate has a lower separation temperature than dark, so requires especially low heating. The safest way to melt chocolate successfully is in a double boiler or in a heatproof bowl suspended over a pan of simmering water or in a microwave or oven at a low temperature. A simple but effective way to speed up the chocolate melting process is by chopping it into small pieces or grinding it in a food processor.

When working with melted chocolate, it is very important to prevent it from coming into contact with water, as this causes it to "seize" and stiffen into a thick paste. Similarly, remember when using chocolate as a coating that it will stick only to ingredients with a dry surface.

Right: A coating of dark chocolate being poured on a dome of chocolate truffle and a biscuit base

Making chocolate truffles

This simple recipe for handmade truffles produces very rich-tasting truffles. This recipe adds a touch of alcohol, a traditional flavoring for truffles, but feel free to experiment with other flavorings, such as coffee or vanilla extract. Bear in mind, though, that you'd need only a few drops of a strong-tasting extract. Vary the coating ingredients, as listed in the recipe, for added visual variety.

½ cup heavy cream

7 oz. dark bittersweet chocolate (70% cocoa solids), broken into small pieces

1 teaspoon rum, brandy, Cointreau, or Grand Marnier

2–3 tablespoons confectioners' sugar, sifted, for coating

2–3 tablespoons cocoa powder, sifted, for coating

2–3 tablespoons finely chopped hazelnuts, for coating

Equipment needed

double boiler

hand-held mixer

Makes 12–16

1 Place the cream in a small pan, bring to the boil, then remove from the heat and set aside until tepid. Meanwhile, place the chocolate in a double boiler or a large heatproof bowl over a pan filled with simmering water, and heat gently until melted, stirring now and then with a wooden spoon.

2 Once the chocolate has melted, remove the bowl (or upper part of the double boiler) from the heat. Gradually add in the tepid cream, stirring as you do so. Stir in the rum or other alcohol, mixing well.

3 Using a hand-held mixer, aerate the chocolate mixture by whisking it for a few minutes until it becomes lighter and stands up in soft peaks.

4 Take large teaspoonfuls of the truffle mixture and shape it into rough balls with your fingers.

5 Coat the truffles in the confectioners' sugar, cocoa, or chopped hazelnuts. Store in a lidded container in the refrigerator for up to three days. Remove an hour before eating to soften them slightly.

Making classic fudge

Invented in the 1880s, in the United States, these creamy, succulent squares are still popular. Try varying the basic recipe with cherries, nuts, rum and raisins, or vanilla.

1¼ cups condensed milk

⅝ cup milk

2¼ cups brown crystal sugar

1 stick butter

Equipment needed

shallow baking pan
(about 12 x 8 in.)

candy thermometer

Makes approx 1½ lb.

1 Put all the ingredients into a large nonstick saucepan. Heat gently, stirring with a wooden spoon, until all the sugar has dissolved. Bring to the boil and simmer gently for 10–15 minutes, stirring continuously until the temperature reaches 240°F on a candy thermometer or test using the "soft ball" method (see page 86). Lightly grease the baking pan and line with baking parchment.

2 Remove the pan from the heat. Beat the mixture with a wooden spoon for 5–10 minutes, until it is thick and grainy and the shine is taken off.

3 Pour the fudge mixture into the tin. Use a sharp knife to score the surface into squares, taking care not to cut all the way through. When cool, cut into squares and remove from the tin. Fudge can be stored in an airtight container for up to a month.

For a different flavor, try adding the following ingredients at the beating stage:

Fruit & Nut: Add ¼ scant cup chopped glacé cherries and ⅜ cup chopped pecans.
Rum & Raisin: Stir in 2 tablespoons dark rum mixed with ¾ cup chopped raisins.
Vanilla: Replace the brown crystal sugar with superfine sugar and add 1 teaspoon vanilla extract.

Making simple syrup

Also called stock syrup, this is made from sugar and water and, when heated to different temperatures, is the starting point for many different confectionery items, ranging from fluffy marshmallows to brittle lollipops. It is also used to soak sponges for desserts or for preserving fruit. Once cooled, the syrup can be flavored with alcohol or lemon juice.

Sugar Temperature Stages and Usage

Name	Temperature	Description	Usage
Thread	223–235°F	The syrup drips from a spoon, forming thin threads in water.	Glacé and candied fruits
Soft ball	235–245°F	The syrup easily forms a ball while in the cold water, but flattens once removed.	Fudge and fondant
Firm ball	245–250°F	The syrup is formed into a stable ball, but loses its round shape once pressed.	Caramel candies
Hard ball	250–266°F	The syrup holds its ball shape, but remains sticky.	Divinity and marshmallows
Soft crack	270–290°F	The syrup will form firm but pliable threads.	Nougat and taffy
Hard crack	300–310°F	The syrup will crack if you try to mold it.	Brittles and lollipops
Caramel	320–350°F	The sugar syrup will turn golden.	Pralines

2 cups superfine sugar

2 cups water

Makes a little less than 3 cups

1 Simply pour the water into a small saucepan, then add the sugar, so that the sugar can start to dissolve without burning.

2 Bring to the boil and simmer for 4–5 minutes, then remove from the heat and leave to cool. If you are adding alcohol, wait until the syrup has cooled, otherwise it will just evaporate. The syrup can be stored in a sealed jar or bottle in the refrigerator for a month.

Making marshmallows

These vanilla-flavored marshmallows are a real treat—definitely a cut above the mass-produced version.

Making marshmallows is very rewarding and great fun for all the family—the children can help with the final whisking once the mixture has cooled to a safe temperature. It's not a quick candy to make, but it is well worth the effort! They are delicious dipped in a warm chocolate sauce with strawberries or just eaten by themselves.

vegetable oil

⅜ (rounded) cup sifted confectioners' sugar

⅜ (rounded) cup sifted cornstarch

9 sheets of leaf gelatin or 2 slightly rounded tablespoons of powdered gelatin

water (for amount see instructions)

2 cups superfine sugar

1 tablespoon liquid glucose or light corn syrup

2 large egg whites

1 teaspoon vanilla extract

Equipment needed

shallow baking pan (about 12 x 8 in.)

candy thermometer

metal pitcher

electric whisk (optional)

Makes 30

1 Lightly grease the tray with a little vegetable oil and dust it with half of the confectioners' sugar and cornstarch. Soak the leaf gelatin in ⅝ cup cold water.

2 Put ¼ cup water, superfine sugar and liquid glucose (or corn syrup) into a heavy-based pan. Bring to the boil and continue cooking for about 12 to 15 minutes until the mixture reaches the hard ball stage (see page 86). When the syrup is up to temperature, carefully add in the softened gelatin sheets and their soaking water. The syrup will bubble up, so take care not to burn yourself. Pour the syrup into a metal pitcher.

3 Whisk the egg whites until stiff, preferably with an electric whisk in a mixing bowl. Continue whisking while pouring in the hot syrup from the pitcher. The mixture will become shiny and start to thicken. Add the vanilla extract and continue whisking for about 5–10 minutes, until the mixture is stiff and thick enough to hold its shape on the whisk.

4 Pour the mixture into the prepared tin and smooth with a wet spatula if necessary to remove any peaks. Leave for at least an hour to set. If you want to cover the tray, use a food sack, as plastic wrap or foil will stick and you will lose some of your marshmallow.

5 Dust the work surface and the marshmallow with some of the remaining confectioners' sugar and cornstarch. Loosen the marshmallow around the sides of the tray with a spatula, and then turn it out onto the dusted surface. Cut into squares and roll in the sugar and cornstarch. Leave to dry a little on a wire rack. To serve, carefully place the marshmallows onto skewers and serve with warm chocolate sauce. The marshmallows can be stored in an airtight container in a cabinet for up to two weeks.

Using your produce

Candied orange peel

These are lovely to make, and the aroma of the cooking oranges makes this a perfect winter activity. They also make great Christmas presents when tied together in bunches with pretty ribbon. The sugar syrup used here is a variation on the basic simple syrup used in many confectionery recipes (see page 87).

4 large oranges
1¼ scant cups superfine sugar, plus extra for coating
4 cups water
10 oz. dark bittersweet chocolate (70% cocoa solids)

Makes about 60

1 Score the oranges into quarters using either a sharp knife or a citrus scorer. Peel the oranges carefully, trying to keep the peels intact. Set the orange flesh aside and use in a separate recipe. Using a sharp knife, cut away as much of the white pith from the peels as possible — don't worry if some remains. Slice the peel lengthwise into strips approximately ⅜ in. wide.

2 Put the sugar and water in a saucepan over medium heat and boil for 5 minutes. Add the strips of peel and reduce the heat to a slow simmer on the lowest setting. Do not stir. Simmer gently for 2 hours until the syrup reduces to approximately one-quarter of its original volume. Remove the saucepan from the heat and allow the mixture to cool. Once cooled, drain the peels.

3 Preheat the oven to a very low temperature, approximately 200°F. Put some superfine sugar in a bowl and dip the peels in the sugar, coating them evenly. Place them on a baking sheet lined with baking parchment and sprinkle with more sugar if necessary.

4 Place the peels in the cool oven for an hour to allow them to dry out. Check at 20-minute intervals to make sure that the peels aren't cooking. Alternatively, leave on a drying rack overnight. Once the peels are completely dry, scrape off any excess sugar clumps.

5 Put the chocolate in a double boiler or a small bowl set over a saucepan of gently simmering water. Don't let the bowl touch the water. Heat gently until the chocolate has melted. Dip each piece of peel in turn into the chocolate at least halfway, then place the chocolate-coated peel strips on a wire rack and leave to set. Store in an airtight container.

Figs in vanilla syrup

These gorgeous fruits look magnificent in the jar, beautifully pink and jewel-like. Baking the jar in the oven will help the figs to keep. The syrup used here is another variation on the simple syrup (see page 87), only this time it is scented with vanilla and cinnamon.

¼ scant cup granulated sugar

½ vanilla bean

1-inch cinnamon stick

1 scant cup water

6–7 figs, halved

¼ teaspoon citric acid

Fills a 1-pint jar

1 Preheat the oven to 300°F. Place the sugar, vanilla bean, and cinnamon stick in a pan and add the water. Stir over a low heat to dissolve the sugar, then bring to the boil and simmer for two minutes to make a syrup. Remove from the heat. Discard the cinnamon stick. Slice the vanilla bean in half lengthwise, scrape out the seeds with a knife, and add them to the syrup.

2 Pack the figs into a clean sterilized jar (see page 121) with the cut sides facing outward. Push the vanilla bean halves among the figs. Pour the syrup over the figs to fill the jar, swiveling the jar to remove any air bubbles.

3 Wrap aluminum foil over the top of the jar and place it in the oven, on a baking tray lined with several layers of folded newspaper. Bake for 25–30 minutes, by which time the syrup will have turned a lovely shade of pink. Remove from the oven, discard the foil, and seal tightly.

S'mores

This is one for the kids. S'mores are an American campfire classic, in which graham crackers, toasted marshmallows, and chocolate squares are sandwiched together to make a delicious, gooey taste sensation. You can use a cookie, such as langue de chat or almond thin, instead of graham crackers, although really any plain cookie will do. You're bound to want "some mores."

16 graham crackers
8 pieces of dark semisweet chocolate
16 marshmallows (see page 89)

Equipment needed
8 metal skewers

Serves 4

1 Put half the cookies on a plate, and top each one with a square of chocolate.

2 Preheat a barbecue. Thread two marshmallows onto each skewer and cook over hot coals for about two minutes, turning constantly until the marshmallows are melted and toasted to your taste; some like them golden-brown, some like them black. Remove from the heat and leave to cool slightly.

3 Put the marshmallows onto the chocolate squares and sandwich together with the remaining cookies. Gently ease out the skewers and serve the s'mores as soon as the chocolate has melted.

Chocolate chili-salted truffles

A spicy take on the traditional truffle, these salty chili chocolate versions, rolled in Himalayan pink rock salt, are so divine you won't be able to stop eating them! The recipe is a variation on the classic chocolate truffle (see page 82), using butter instead of some of the cream.

½ lb. dark semisweet chocolate (70% cocoa solids), roughly chopped
¼ cup light cream
1 tablespoon unsalted butter
½ teaspoon confectioners' chili oil (or more or less, depending on taste)

For the salted cocoa dusting powder
¼ cup superfine sugar
⅛ rounded cup sifted cocoa powder
1 teaspoon ground cinnamon
1 tablespoon Himalayan pink rock salt

Equipment needed
melon baller

Makes 40

1 Put the chocolate, cream, and butter in a heatproof bowl.

2 Place the bowl over a pan of simmering water, making sure the water does not touch the bottom of the bowl. Once the chocolate has started to melt, stir gently until the mixture is smooth and creamy.

3 Stir in the chili oil and pour the mixture into a shallow bowl. Refrigerate until firm.

4 To make the dusting powder, mix together the superfine sugar, cocoa powder, cinnamon, and Himalayan salt in a bowl.

5 When the chocolate mixture has set, scoop out small amounts with a melon baller and roll into balls. Toss the truffles in the dusting powder and serve.

White and black puddings

These may be desserts, rather than candies, but hiding in the middle of each of these indulgent delights is a creamier version of the chocolate truffle mixture (see page 82). Once baked, it turns into molten chocolate, making a dramatic contrast with the white chocolate sponge pudding that surrounds it. It is very important to use the best-quality white and dark chocolate you can find.

For the dark chocolate filling

2¼ oz. dark bittersweet chocolate (70% cocoa solids), chopped

⅓ cup heavy cream

For the white chocolate sponge

3½ oz. white chocolate, chopped

1½ sticks unsalted butter, at room temperature

⅝ cup (rounded) superfine sugar

3 large eggs, beaten

1¾ cups self-rising flour

pinch of salt

½ teaspoon vanilla extract

about 4 tablespoons milk

Equipment needed

ice cube tray

6 small (3-in. diameter) dariole molds

whipped cream, to serve

Serves 6

1 Oil six holes of the ice cube tray. Put the dark chocolate in the top of a double boiler or a heatproof bowl set over a pan of simmering water; melt gently (do not let the base of the bowl touch the water). Remove the bowl from the heat and stir until just smooth. Stir in the cream, then pour into the oiled holes in the ice cube tray to make six "cubes." Freeze for at least an hour.

2 Preheat the oven to 350°F. Grease the dariole molds.

3 When you are ready to make the pudding, melt the white chocolate as above. When melted and smooth, leave to cool.

4 First sift the flour. Put the butter in a bowl and beat until creamy, then gradually beat in the sugar. When the mixture is very light and fluffy, beat in the eggs, 1 tablespoon at a time, beating well after each addition. Using a large metal spoon, carefully fold in the flour and salt, then the melted chocolate, vanilla extract, and just enough milk to give the mixture a firm dropping consistency. Spoon into the prepared molds to fill by about half. Turn out the dark chocolate cubes, put one into the center of each mold, then fill with more sponge mixture to three-quarters full.

5 Stand the molds in a roasting pan, cover loosely with well-buttered foil, and bake for 25 minutes, or until just firm to the touch. Run a round-bladed knife inside each mold to loosen the puddings, then carefully turn out onto individual plates. Serve with whipped cream.

Note: The chocolate filling should be made at least an 1 hour before making the sponge, and can be kept in the freezer for up to a week.

Chocolate maple fudge

This variation on the classic recipe (see page 84) is a rich and decadent fudge for those with the sweetest of teeth, to serve as a pick-me-up with mid-morning coffee or after dinner with a chocolate liqueur. Nibble a chunk and let it melt on your tongue—heaven! If you don't have a candy thermometer, boil the sugar mixture for 5–7 minutes to the "soft ball" stage (see page 86).

2¼ cups turbinado sugar

⅜ cup maple syrup

⅝ cup milk or cream

1¼ sticks unsalted butter, cubed

5 oz. dark bittersweet chocolate (60–70% cocoa solids), broken into pieces

2 teaspoons vanilla extract

salt crystals

Equipment needed

candy thermometer (for best results)

shallow 6 x 9-in. (or similar size) baking pan

Makes 54 1-in. squares

1 Have a large bowl of cold water ready in the sink. Grease the tin.

2 Put the sugar, maple syrup, milk, butter, and chocolate in a large, heavy-based pan and stir over gentle heat, without boiling, until the sugar has dissolved.

3 Bring the mixture to the boil and boil hard until you reach 240°F on a candy thermometer, stirring every now and then to prevent it from sticking.

4 As soon as you reach this temperature, remove the pan from the heat and dip the base in the bowl of cold water to stop the mixture from cooking. Add the vanilla extract and beat well with a wooden spoon until the fudge becomes thick and creamy, with a grainy texture. Pour into the tin, smooth the surface and leave to cool for five minutes. Press some salt crystals all over the fudge.

5 When it is almost set, score squares in the surface of the fudge with the tip of a sharp knife. When completely cold, turn out and cut into squares.

Variation: For a nutty alternative, fold in 1 cup chopped walnuts or pecans immediately after beating the fudge.

Jewel-colored lollipops

These lollipops are great fun. They use another variation on the simple syrup (see page 87), this time using very little water so they harden up nicely. You don't have to make them with molds: when the sugar cools slightly, it becomes easy to mold into any shape. A fantastic treat for children!

⅞ cup granulated sugar

¼ cup liquid glucose or light corn syrup

food colorings

food flavorings, such as lemon juice, orange blossom water, strawberry flavoring, peppermint flavoring, or rose water

Equipment needed

lollipop molds and sticks

candy thermometer

Makes about 16 depending on the size of the mold

1 Wash, dry, and butter the lollipop molds, if using. If you don't have molds, you can use a silicone sheet or buttered waxed paper.

2 Mix the sugar, liquid glucose or corn syrup, and 4 tablespoons of water in a saucepan. Cook over a medium heat, stirring with a wooden spoon until the mixture comes to the boil. To prevent sugar crystallization, use a pastry brush dipped in cold water and brush down the sides of the pan at regular intervals.

3 Boil the mixture without stirring until it reaches 300°F on a candy thermometer. Remove from the heat. Mix in a few drops of food coloring and any flavoring: use 1 tablespoon of lemon juice for the yellow lollies, 1 tablespoon of orange blossom water for the orange lollies, and 1 tablespoon of strawberry flavoring for the red lollies.

4 Put the lollipop sticks into the molds and then carefully pour the mixture into each mold, ensuring that it doesn't spill over the top. If you don't have molds, use a teaspoon gently to spoon and shape a lollipop on a silicone sheet or waxed paper. Set aside and leave to cool at room temperature.

5 If storing, wrap the lollipops individually in cellophane or waxed paper and place in an airtight container.

Rocky road sundae

This voluptuous combination of nuts, chocolate, marshmallows, and glacé cherries is the perfect pick-me-up for anyone with the blues. Said to have been designed originally to cheer people up during the Great Depression of the 1930s, this sundae is guaranteed to bring a smile to your guests' faces.

For the chocolate sauce
2 tablespoons corn syrup
³⁄₈ cup heavy cream
3½ oz. dark bittersweet chocolate
2 tablespoons unsalted butter

For the marshmallow ice cream
3 cups vanilla ice cream
¾ cup chopped marshmallows (see page 89)
4 cups chopped glacé cherries
½ cup toasted coconut flakes

For the chocolate crunch ice cream
3 cups chocolate ice cream
I cup crushed chocolate cookies
½ (rounded) cup salted peanuts

To finish
chocolate vermicelli, to sprinkle
halved glacé cherries, to decorate

Equipment needed
4 glass sundae dishes

Serves 4

1 For the chocolate sauce, place the syrup, cream, chocolate, and butter together in a heavy-based saucepan and whisk over a gentle heat until the chocolate has melted and the sauce is smooth and glossy. Leave to cool.

2 To make the marshmallow ice cream, take the vanilla ice cream from the freezer and leave it to soften slightly. Once the ice cream is pliable, stir in the marshmallows, cherries, and coconut flakes. Put ice cream back in the freezer if not using immediately.

3 To make the chocolate crunch ice cream, take the chocolate ice cream from the freezer and leave it to soften slightly. Once the ice cream is pliable, stir in the crushed chocolate cookies and peanuts. Put ice cream back in the freezer if not using immediately.

4 To assemble, put scoops of the marshmallow ice cream in the sundae dishes. Drizzle some of the chocolate sauce over (warmed if liked), and add a scoop of chocolate crunch ice cream, followed by a second scoop of marshmallow ice cream. Sprinkle with chocolate vermicelli and decorate with a few glacé cherries. Serve immediately.

Chapter 4

THE PANTRY

The pantry, with its shelves lined with neatly labeled jars of colorful, homemade preserves, is an iconic image of housekeeping that still appeals. Throughout history, people have sought ways in which to store and keep precious foodstuffs, especially when they were abundantly available, transforming them from perishable fresh ingredients into foods that could last through the lean times. Preserving's traditional imperative, therefore, has always been to make the most of seasonal plenty. Preserving foods also transformed them, affecting their flavor and texture, and these preserved foods, of course, also became appreciated and enjoyed in their own right, used to add relish to the dishes we eat. A piece of farmhouse cheese with chutney, cold meat, and pickles, bread with strawberry jam; many of our favorite food pairings feature preserved foods.

Five types of ingredients, each with preserving qualities, play a pivotal part in making preserves: vinegar, salt, oil, sugar, and spices. Vinegar, which occurs naturally as wine sours, hence its name (derived from the French *vin aigre*, meaning "sour wine"), has long been used as a preservative due to its acid content. Pickling foods in vinegar is a way of preserving food that was known by the ancient Egyptians and Babylonians and used by the Greeks and Romans. Apicius, the famous Roman epicure, wrote of many different types of pickles, and they were much esteemed by wealthy Romans, as was garum, a condiment made from fermented fish. Verjus, the acid liquid made from green grapes, was also used by the Romans as a pickling medium. Another traditional preserving medium is the family of wine and spirits, with fruit preserved in alcohol a classic delicacy.

Salt's remarkable preserving properties make it a valuable ingredient in prolonging the length of time during which foods can be eaten safely, and foods have long been salted in order to keep them. Salted cabbage, made during the Middle Ages, is the precursor of sauerkraut, created by fermenting salted cabbage. Salting ingredients first, by using either dry salt (known as dry-curing) or brine—a liquid salt solution—(known as brine-curing), before immersing them in vinegar, is a traditional stage in pickling. The salt is used to preserve the food, add flavor, and draw out excess moisture. Brine is also a preserving medium in its own right, with gherkins, for example, being traditionally cured in brine. There is also an ancient tradition of preserving pickled ingredients in oil.

When it came to making sweet preserves, honey rather than sugar, was the original sweetener, with the ancient Greeks and Romans preserving foods, such as quinces, in honey. Because sugar was a costly ingredient for many centuries, preserves made with large amounts of sugar, such as jam, were a luxury until well into the nineteenth century.

Spices, noted for their keeping qualities, and herbs have long been used to add flavor to preserves such

as pickles, chutneys, and jelly. The range of spices and herbs available allows for a wide range of flavors. Piquancy can be created by adding chilies, mustard seeds, or peppercorns, for example, with fragrant herbs such as bay leaves, rosemary, or tarragon each adding their own specific aroma and flavor. Spices are used either whole or ground, depending on the level of flavoring required, with whole spices adding a milder flavor than ground ones, especially freshly ground spices. However, the advantage of adding whole spices, such as cloves, peppercorns, and cinnamon sticks, to preserves such as flavored vinegars is that they do not cloud the liquid in the way that ground spices do, making a lovely clear preserve.

Nowadays, we have become used to buying many foods that would have been made at home just a couple of generations ago. There is something rather appealing about

making chili sauce or strawberry jam in your own kitchen at home, using good-quality ingredients and experimenting with flavors, rather than buying a mass-produced version from a supermarket. Artisanal producers of preserves know the value of producing foods such as jams or chutneys in small batches, because this domestic scale of production allows you to keep a close eye on the making process and so ensure good results. Even today, in our age of plentiful food supplies and deep freezers, there is still a profound satisfaction to the process of transforming, say, a glut of ripe tomatoes into tomato sauce or turning windfall apples into chutneys to be enjoyed in the months ahead.

Above left: Rosemary-infused olive oil
Above right: Apricots in syrup spiced with vanilla and cinnamon
Left: Mozzarella and tomatoes preserved in oil

Preserving fruits and vegetables

Our rich, centuries-long heritage of preserving fruits and vegetables has produced many ways to do this: pickles, chutneys, jams, marmalades, jellies, ketchups, cordials, and fruit cheeses among them. Home preserving offers the home cook considerable opportunity for creativity, with the chance to create numerous diffferent flavors with the same basic ingredients, depending on which herbs, spices, sugar, or vinegar are used.

Pickles

A traditional way of preserving food, popular with both the ancient Greeks and Romans, is by pickling it in a solution with either a high acid or salt content, since both acid and salt discourage microbial growth and so act as effective preserving mediums. Vinegar and brine are the two major pickling solutions. The traditional method of pickling vegetables in vinegar involves them first being sprinkled generously with salt or placed in brine to draw out their

moisture, a process that helps the vegetables retain their texture and also reduces the risk of bacterial development. The vegetables are then rinsed to wash off the salt, covered with either hot or cold vinegar, and stored. In order for the vinegar to pickle effectively, it should have at least 5 percent acetic acid content. The choice of hot or cold vinegar depends on the texture desired, with the cold vinegar method producing crunchier pickles than the hot vinegar method. Extra flavor is created by the addition of spices, herbs, and aromatics, such as peppercorns, cloves, bay leaves, tarragon, garlic, and onion, to the vinegar.

Chutneys

Vinegar also plays a key part in chutneys, with sugar being another important ingredient in these. The word "chutney," which derives from the Indian word *chatni*, is used in the Western kitchen to mean a cooked preserve made from chopped vegetables or fruit or a mixture of both, cooked with sugar and vinegar. Long, slow cooking to enhance flavor and reduce down is often a characteristic of chutneys, as is a sour-sweet flavor and a thick texture. Bear in mind, when judging whether your chutney has cooked down enough, that it will thicken as it cools. Another characteristic of chutneys is that they should usually be matured for several weeks in order to allow them to develop in flavor.

Left: Pickled shallots in spiced vinegar
Right: A selection of jams, curds, and marmalades

Meet the producer: Wendy Brandon

Having started her jam making 25 years ago, producing six sugar-free chutneys, made using concentrated apple juice, for a health food cooperative in Brighton, Wendy has expanded her range considerably to around 200 preserves, including jams, jellies, marmalades, and chutneys. Despite offering so many products, Wendy and her team produce her preserves in the way one would cook them at home.

"We make very small batches by hand," explains Wendy. "The reason for cooking jams and marmalades in small batches is that they cook quicker, and quick cooking is important so that they keep their flavor and color, to make a fresh-tasting preserve. I made up my mind from the beginning that even if I expanded, I wasn't going to change how I made my jam. I had no ambition to run a factory."

Wendy carefully sources her ingredients, using "old-fashioned flavorful" fruit varieties where possible and dried fruit as well as fresh in her chutneys, because of their "concentrated" flavor. "Our marmalade isn't too sweet; I use a mixture of sugar and concentrated apple juice, and the apple juice gives a sharper flavor. Making a jam is like making a three-legged stool; you've got to get the balance right between the sugar, the pectin, and the acid content. It took a lot of trial and error to get my recipes right." On making jams at home, Wendy advises testing, "The home cook often makes the mistake of looking at a pan of boiling jam that's liquid and cooking it for longer, but if you do that, you'll end up with a product that cracks teeth! You have to do a setting test. With time, you get a feel for the look of the jam, of how it bubbles and spits." Careful cooking is key to all her production. "We simmer the chutneys for three to four hours, depending on the fruit. They must be properly cooked, as you want all the elements—the fruit,

vegetables, dried fruit, vinegar, sugar, spices, and garlic—to come together as a whole. We fill our jars by hand, rather than using a filling machine, as many people do, and this means we can keep our chutneys chunkier, with more texture. Some people also add starch to their chutneys to make them pass through the filling machine, but that would dull the flavor, so it's something I would never do myself. So many mass-produced chutneys are so bland tasting; people seem frightened of flavor."

Meet the producer: Seafares

Seafares, a company specializing in producing both cooked and raw-cured seafood, is the brainwave of former chef and restaurateur Nigel Bloxham. Nigel uses a method called sott'olio, traditionally used for both seafood and vegetables. The idea came from Nigel's experience in the fish business.

"I saw all this cuttlefish going out to Italy, then the Italians selling it back to [Britain] preserved in oil in jars and thought that someone should do that here," says Nigel. "We use an age-old way of preserving, which is particularly associated with the Mediterranean. Hundreds of years ago, when they wanted to keep wine good, people would simply pour a layer of olive oil over the top to seal it. Now, we didn't have a lot of oil in England, but we had butter, which we used in the same way, pouring it over food when the butter was liquid and letting it solidify and set to form a layer on top, so making potted meats and potted shrimps. It's all about keeping out the air. We use this method with rapeseed [canola] oil, which is a very healthy oil, mixed with a little olive oil for flavor."

Besides the oil, vinegar is an important ingredient in the process. "To help the food keep, you need a product with a pH content, that is an acid content, and for that we use white wine vinegar or cider vinegar," explains Nigel. "Using good-quality seafood is the starting point. We're in a great part of the world for sourcing really good, fresh seafood, with Brixham very close and the rest of Devon and Cornwall nearby. We produce cold-cured seafood including sprats, sardines, and mackerel using the escabeche or sousing method, where raw seafood is covered in wine vinegar so that the vinegar 'cooks' it. It is then covered with oil and sold as a chilled product. Our other products are hot-cooked in wine vinegar, then preserved in oil. You need to cook the seafood enough for the vinegar to penetrate, but not to overcook it, as otherwise it becomes tough. Depending on what we're making and which method we're using, the marinating stage can be just a few hours or a few days. When it comes to flavoring, we use very little salt and we sometimes add herbs or use herb vinegars. We're particularly known for our seafood salad, which is a mixture of cuttlefish, octopus, squid, prawns, mussels, and clams with roasted red pepper."

Ketchups

Today, one of the most familiar table condiments is mass-produced tomato ketchup. The word "ketchup" derives from the Chinese *ke-tsiap*, meaning a fermented fish sauce, and later came to mean a salty, liquid condiment with a long shelf life. Ketchups can be made from fruits, vegetables, and nuts and range in texture from thick to thin. As with chutneys, both sugar and vinegar are often key ingredients in ketchups, with the addition of spices and aromatics such as onion, garlic, or ginger used to create flavor.

Sott'olio

(seafood and vegetables preserved in oil)

Oil's preserving qualities have long been appreciated, and there is an established tradition of preserving foods in oil, usually olive oil—a process the Italians call sott'olio, which means "under oil." Both seafood and vegetables such as artichokes, peppers, mushrooms, and eggplants are popularly stored in this way, with the process involving first cooking the seafood or vegetables, usually by boiling them in vinegar, then cooling them, then covering them all with oil. It's very important that the oil cover the ingredients thoroughly, as otherwise there's a chance of decay occurring. Ingredients preserved in this way have a subtle richness of flavor, and in Italian cuisine they are often served as an antipasto dish. The British tradition of "potting" food in fat, rather than oil, is discussed in The Butcher's chapter on page 140.

Flavored vinegars and oils

Vinegar and oil, both key ingredients in preserving, can also be used as the base for making flavored vinegars and oils, infused with herbs, spices, fruit, and other flavorings, such as garlic. Flavored vinegar is made by steeping the flavoring ingredients in the vinegar for around four weeks until it takes on the required taste. Popular flavoring choices for vinegars include herbs such as tarragon, sage, thyme, or mint and bush fruits, such as raspberries or blackberries. These flavored vinegars are then used in salad dressings. Fruit vinegars can also be diluted with water to make a refreshing drink. Flavored oils are made by adding spices, such as dried chilies, or dried herbs, to a good-quality oil, such as an extra-virgin olive oil, and setting it aside to infuse for around four weeks. Depending on their flavoring, these oils are then used in dressings or as culinary oils.

Bottled fruits

In addition to being used in pickles, chutneys, and ketchups, fruit can be preserved in a number of ways. Bottling fruits in a sugar syrup is a traditional way to store them; however, as with all preserving processes, care must be taken to follow the cooking instructions carefully. Another simple way to preserve fruit is to immerse them in alcohol with sugar, with cherries in brandy a classic example. This has the advantage of not only creating deliciously tipsy fruit but also transforming the alcohol by infusing it with the flavor of the fruit. Generally speaking, firm-textured fruits such as cherries, pears, or peaches, rather than soft berries such as strawberries, give the best results.

Above: A jar of carrot confit
Opposite: Nigel Bloxham uses only the freshest seafood, caught daily, in his sott'olio produce

Jam

Jam, made by cooking fruit with sugar, is probably the most everyday way in which we consume a fruit-based preserve. Other than fruit and sugar, the third essential element needed for jam is pectin, a carbohydrate that occurs naturally in fruits, which causes them to set. Certain fruits, including apples, quinces, and citrus fruits, are rich in pectin, whereas others, such as strawberries and raspberries, are low in pectin. Another variable is that pectin levels vary according to the degree of ripeness, being at their highest just before fruits fully ripen. There is a long tradition of using high-pectin fruits to make jams, and jams made from citrus fruits are traditionally known as "marmalades," with bitter Seville orange marmalade being the best known of these. High-pectin fruits can also be added to low-pectin fruits, either whole or in juice form, to make a jam set. Lemon juice, which has a high pectin content, is often used in this way. Orange seeds are another

useful source of pectin when making jams, and are traditionally used in marmalades. The texture of these marmalades can also be varied according to how thickly the peel is cut.

The process of making jam consists of first gently cooking the fruit in order to soften it, then adding in sugar, cooking it until the sugar has thoroughly dissolved, then boiling the mixture until the jam is ready to set. Other sweeteners, such as concentrated apple juice or apricot purée, can be substituted for sugar. The standard ratio of fruit to sugar is one to one, but this can be tweaked to taste; many artisanal jam makers prefer a higher ratio of fruit in order to create a fruitier flavor. Some recipes suggest warming the sugar before adding it to the fruit to help it dissolve more quickly; this is easily done by placing the sugar in a cool oven (275°F) for a few minutes before adding it to the fruit. The skillful part of making jam

Meet the producer: England Preserves

Noted for its artisanal jams and chutneys, England Preserves was set up in London in 2000 by partners Kai Knutsen and Sky Cracknell.

"We grew up in homes where people made jams and we took what we did for ourselves and turned it into a business," explains Kai. "Essentially what we do is use a very high percentage of fruit. Most industrial jams are boiled for a long time, whereas we simply heat our jams to 90°C [194°F] to sterilize them and to increase their keeping properties. What we're trying to do is to keep the character and color of the fruit. The flavor of fruit is incredibly delicate, and if you boil the jam, you destroy that flavor. It's more of a modern style of jam making, rather than the traditional way of boiling things to death." They take the same approach to their chutneys, cooking them for less time than is traditional.

"We harvest and blast-freeze our fruit, then make the jams in small batches using a steam-jacket kettle, which allows us to monitor the heat very precisely. Each batch will vary a little and requires attention when cooking. We make a gooseberry and elderflower jam, and you have to be careful not to let the elderflower overpower the gooseberry and also not to overcook it, so as to keep that very special gooseberry flavor. As an artisan food maker, you're nurturing something from nature, not stamping industrial parameters on it. The jams we sell are no more than a month old, and we like people to eat them when they're fresh, but the chutneys need a few months for the vinegar to mellow."

As their company name suggests, they work primarily with English fruit, apart from French apricots and Spanish Seville oranges for their marmalade. So committed are they to sourcing locally that they are now growing their own quince trees, from which to make their rich-tasting quince cheese. "We met a lot of farmers through working on farmers' markets, so we have a network of growers that we use. Our damson jam is made with a mixture of damson varieties. It's my favorite of our jams. It has the sweetness of jam and the fruity sharpness of damsons; a beautiful taste of England."

rests in pulling off the boiling stage successfully and this is where timing is vital. If the jam is not boiled for long enough, it will be too runny; whereas if it is boiled for too long, it will darken and caramelize. There are a number of ways of testing when jam has reached this setting point. The plate test involves spooning a small amount of the jam onto a chilled plate. If the jam sets and forms a skin that wrinkles when pushed, the jam is ready. Alternatively, test the jam using a pre-warmed candy thermometer; 221°F is the temperature at which the jam will set.

Above left: The sharpness of gooseberry jam makes it a great savory accompaniment
Above right: Pear jam with vanilla seeds dotted throughout
Right: Mixed fruit, or tutti frutti, jam

Jelly

Another type of fruit preserve requiring the presence of pectin is jelly, often made with fruits naturally high in pectin such as red currants or apples. The process of making a jelly from fruit is a slow one, since the juice must first be extracted from the fruit. To do this, the fruit is cooked with a little water until it has softened and released its juices. The cooked fruit mixture is then placed in a very fine muslin bag, known as a jelly bag, suspended over a container, and left to allow its juice to drip out, usually overnight. Do not be tempted to speed up this dripping process by squeezing the bag, as this results in cloudy jelly rather than the desired clear, sparkling jelly. The juice is then measured and sugar added to it, with 1 cup sugar to 1¼ cups fruit juice being a usual ratio. This mixture is gently heated until the sugar has dissolved, then, as with jam, brought to the boil and boiled until it reaches setting point, which is the same as for jam.

Fruit butters and cheeses

Whole fruits, rather than their extracted juice, are the starting point for making the sweetened fruit purées known as fruit butters and fruit cheeses. A fruit butter, as its name suggests, is a fruit purée with a spreadable texture, whereas the term "fruit cheese" refers to a fruit purée so thick that it has a solid, sliceable texture; Spanish membrillo, made from quinces, is an example. In fact, the fruit pulp left over after making a fruit jelly can be used to make these, as can overripe fruits that are too ripe to use for jams or jellies. The fruit is cooked until soft, sieved if needed, to remove any skin or seeds, then cooked with sugar until reduced and thickened. The ratio of sugar to fruit for a fruit butter is 1 cup sugar to 2 cups fruit pulp, while for a fruit cheese it is 1 cup sugar to 1 cup fruit pulp. Typical fruits for these preserves include plums, damsons, quinces, and apples, all fruits naturally high in pectin.

Fruit syrups

Fruit can also be used to make traditional fruit syrups: fruit-flavored concentrated liquids that can then be diluted to taste. To make a fruit syrup, the fruit needs first to be cooked gently with a little water in order to soften it and release its juices. The fruit mixture is then placed in a jelly bag and left to drip overnight. This juice is then measured, sweetened to taste with sugar, and heated gently until the sugar has dissolved, creating a fruit syrup.

Left: A rose-tinged jelly made from crab apples
Right: In Britain, black currants are one of the most popular fruits to use when making syrups

Sourcing the ingredients

When choosing fruits or vegetables for home preserving, bear in mind that you should choose them at the appropriate state of ripeness for the preserve that you are making. When preserving fruits in alcohol, use barely ripe fruits, because the process will soften them. The best pickles are made with good-quality produce that is ripe, but not overripe. Similarly, fruit for jam should be just ripe, rather than overripe, as otherwise it will be tricky to get the jam to set. Ripe fruits that would be too ripe to use for jam making give the best results for jellies and fruit cheeses, where extracting the juice is the starting point. Chutneys, with their long, slow cooking times, are more accommodating of different degrees of ripeness.

When it comes to choosing fruits and vegetables for home preserving, the use of good-quality produce is important, so pick through the fruits or vegetables that you want to use, discarding any that are damaged or decayed. Seasonality is also a major factor. Using ingredients when they are at their best, most abundant, and cheapest was always the traditional imperative for preserving, and it still is today. Using up fruits and vegetables from your own garden or a neighbor's is a good starting point. Markets are a great source of competitively priced fresh produce, with farmers' markets and farm shops offering a chance to find traditional varieties of fruits and vegetables, grown for their flavor, rather than their cosmetic appearance. Many traditional ingredients for preserves grow wild and can be foraged for free. Fruits such as blackberries, blueberries, and crab apples, for example, are all excellent for use in preserves, and gathering them is a pleasurable outdoor activity.

For preserves that require vinegar, using good-quality vinegar is recommended, so make sure that the vinegar has at least 5 percent acetic acid. Different types of vinegar vary in flavor, with, for example, white wine vinegar far more delicate than malt vinegar, so bear this in mind when choosing which type to use. This also holds true when choosing which sugar to use, as different sugars range considerably in flavor. Preserving sugar is often recommended for jam making as its large crystals make it dissolve slowly and reduce the risk of burning. Jam sugar, known as gelling sugar in the United States, has added pectin and citric acid in it to help the jam set.

Different types of vinegar

Balsamic vinegar This famous Italian vinegar, made from grape juice, is available in both inexpensive, mass-produced versions and costly, artisanal, traditional ones. With its dark color and pronounced sweet flavor, it tends to be used in chutneys such as onion marmalade.

Cider vinegar Made from cider, this vinegar has a distinct apple flavor and is often used for pickling fruits.

Malt vinegar Made from a type of beer created from malted barley, this has a strong flavor and is generally used for pickles, such as pickled onions.

Sherry vinegar Made from sherry, this traditional Spanish vinegar has a distinctive sweet, nutty flavor.

Wine vinegar Made from either white wine or red wine and colored accordingly, their delicate flavor means that wine vinegars are widely used in preserving. Wine vinegars made using the traditional, time-consuming Orleans method, where wine is carefully converted into vinegar in wooden barrels, are particularly esteemed for their depth of flavor.

Opposite: Shallots are the key ingredient for the standard pickled onion

How to store

Scrupulous care must be taken when covering and sealing preserves, which should be stored in clean, heat-sterilized containers (see page 114). Always carefully follow the recipe instructions regarding bottling, storage, and consumption. Bear in mind that food stored in vinegar or alcohol needs to be covered by the liquid in order to be thoroughly preserved. Use a canning funnel to pour the food or liquid into the jar, leaving a "head space" of ½ –1 in. between the food and the rim. Stir the contents with a knife to release any air bubbles, then seal the jars. If sealing with paraffin, follow the manufacturer's instructions. Liquid preserves, such as syrups, stored in bottles with corks will gradually evaporate through the cork, so a wax coating on corks is advised to make them airtight. When using canning jars, do check that any fittings such as rubber rings haven't decayed.

To help keep an accurate record of your creations, label your preserves clearly with the date of making and the contents. The general rule for storing preserves is to keep them somewhere dark, dry, and cool, such as a closet or pantry, well away from a heat source, such as an oven.

Above: Almost any fruit can be preserved in syrup. Here are crab apples, orange slices, figs, and cherries

Making vinegar

Making your own vinegar at home is very simple indeed, with the results so much more flavorful than mass-produced vinegar. Using a fruit juice, such as apple or grape, gives a lovely fruity flavor.

The fruit juice you select should be free of additives or preservatives. Fresh apple or grape juice is a good choice. By using grapes or grape juice, you create wine vinegar. If you use apple juice, you'll end up with cider vinegar. If the fruit juice has less than 10 percent sugars, it will produce less than 5 percen alcohol and less than 4 percent acetic acid in the finished vinegar and will be prone to spoiling.

To ensure success, especially for your first time, start by adding organic unfiltered vinegar from a health-food store, or use a vinegar starter, or "mother," available on the internet. After you have done that once, just reserve a cup or so of your own homemade vinegar to add to the next batch. This is the source of bacteria for the fermentation process.

3 cups "mother" unfiltered vinegar

3 cups fresh fruit juice

Equipment needed

large glass jar or container with a wide mouth (don't use metal or plastic, as the acid can interact with these materials and ruin your vinegar)

piece of muslin

string

coffee filter paper

small bottles with airtight lids

Makes 2½ pints

1 Get yourself a large glass jar with a wide, open neck that will allow you access to the "mother" when it forms. Mix together the vinegar and fruit juice. If the fruit juice is below 10 percent sugar content, add a couple of spoonfuls of sugar. Cover the opening with a double layer of muslin to keep out the fruit flies (but be sure, they will come to it wherever you put it).

3 Keep checking the vinegar until it is as strong as you like it, or It seems to be losing strength. This can be any time from 6 to12 weeks. Reserve some for the next batch.

4 Strain it through some coffee filter paper to remove the "mother." Bottle the vinegar in small bottles with airtight lids to reduce the chance of any residue of the "mother" starting to work again (the bacteria need both food and air). Leave it for at least six months in the back of a closet or cabinet before using (you could use it right away, but by leaving it you will have a smoother taste).

2 Put the mix into a warm, dark place, such as a closet. The temperature should be 75–85°F in the storage area.

Note: When all the alcohol has been used up by the bacteria, they will start to feed on the acetic acid, producing water and carbon dioxide. This is why the vinegar starts to weaken and becomes prone to spoilage. You can stop all the action by pasteurizing the vinegar at 158°F to kill the remaining bacteria of all kinds before bottling.

Pickling vinegars

If you want to produce vinegar for pickling, you will need to be more controlled in your production and will need to add in another stage so you can guarantee the alcohol content. To produce the purest flavored vinegar, you need to produce a good vinegar "stock," "wash," or "substrate," which are the names given to the alcohol mixture used to make vinegar. And the best way to ensure this is to produce a "wine," using a wine-making kit from the fruit first; because the alcohol production is an anaerobic action and vinegar production is aerobic, the two processes need to be separated to keep control of the alcohol production. The most inexpensive way to start producing the vinegar stock is to buy a wine kit, and then you can produce the vinegar stock from many different kinds of garden produce.

Things to remember include the fact that the specific gravity of the juice at the start of the process should between 10 and 18 on the Brix scale and 0 when finished (0 = no sugar left in the vinegar stock). A good kit will contain a Brix hydrometer, which is very easy to use, but you need to follow the instructions closely.

Flavored vinegars

If you want to flavor the vinegar, you can do this by adding your chosen flavor and leaving it to infuse for about six weeks. Never leave items in the vinegar for longer than six weeks, as they can cause the whole thing to spoil.

Some things to try in vinegar:
- raspberries
- strawberries
- blueberries
- chilies
- basil
- onion
- dill
- garlic
- oregano

Using your vinegar

If you attempt to make vinegar at home, you'll develop an appreciation for this ancient art and science, but do be careful. While homemade vinegar can be good for dressing salads and general-purpose use, its acidity may not be adequate for safe use in pickling and canning. Unless you are certain the acidity is at least 4 percent, don't pickle or can with it.

Using canning jars: Special jars, called mason jars, are normally required for preserving—or canning—food. These jars are made of glass that has been tempered to withstand the high temperatures required for sterilization. You can use ordinary glass jars, provided the food is to be consumed within a few weeks. In the United States the way to use these is to pour liquid paraffin on top before applying the lid. In Britain, waxed paper disks are used.

To sterilize mason jars, you will need a water bath canner, which comes with a wire rack to support the jars (or a deep saucepan and a separate wire rack). Wash the jars in hot, soapy water; rinse well and allow to air dry. Put enough water in the canner to come at least 1 in. above the tops of the jars. Bring the water to a rolling boil, then, using tongs, insert the jars, lids, and sealing rings. Keep them submerged in the boiling water for at least five minutes. Remove them with the tongs and allow to air dry on paper towels before inserting the food.

Right: Bottles of homemade cider, red wine, and white wine vinegar
Below: Experiment with different herbs and note the impact they have on the finished flavor

Making green tomato, raisin, and mint chutney

Among all the thousands of chutneys, this is particularly special, as it has a sharp clean flavor, which, unlike many others, is neither too cloying nor too sweet. This recipe is also a useful way of using up unripe or green tomatoes, which are too hard and bitter to be eaten raw and fail to ripen, even if left on a sunny windowsill or wrapped in brown paper bags. As with all chutneys, make sure the ingredients are of a good quality and free of any bruises or blemishes.

3¼ lb. green tomatoes, cut into dice

1 lb. onions, minced

3 cups raisins

2⅜ cups brown sugar

1 cup cider vinegar (see page 112)

½ fresh root ginger, peeled and finely sliced

1 teaspoon cayenne pepper

½ teaspoon salt

1¼ cups coarsely chopped fresh mint leaves

Equipment needed

large saucepan or preserving pan

5 warm, dry sterilized 1-pt. glass jars (see page 114)

Makes 5 x 1 pint jars

1 Put all the ingredients except the mint in a large saucepan or preserving pan and bring to a simmer over medium to low heat. Then leave to simmer uncovered for about 1 hour, stirring occasionally with a wooden spoon, taking care not to crush or break up the vegetables or to let the mixture bubble too fiercely.

2 Stir in the mint and simmer for another 15 minutes, or until the vegetables are just tender but not too soft.

3 Have ready the sterilized glass jars and pack the chutney loosely into them. Place the lids, with the rubber seals, on the jars but do not tighten. Allow the chutney to cool, then seal the lids tightly and label the jars and store them in a cool dark place to mature for about a month before you even think of trying the chutney. Once opened, the chutney will last for at least three months if refrigerated.

Making sott'olio

This classic Mediterranean way of preserving food combines first cooking the ingredients in vinegar then immersing them in olive oil. The results both look and taste fantastic.

Sott'olio requires some care in preparation because although oil has preserving properties, it is not a preservative; it prevents spoilage merely by isolating the vegetables from the air. This means that the vegetables must be fully cooked (often in vinegar, whose acidity acts as a disinfectant) and transferred immediately to a sterile jar, which must be filled immediately, and then tapped briskly so as to dislodge all the air bubbles. Do not pack anything raw in oil, because raw vegetables can harbor bacteria on their surfaces, even if they have been well washed; and some of these bacteria can do quite well in the anaerobic (i.e. airless) environment of a sott'olio jar. In particular, garlic has been known to harbor the bacteria that cause botulism. Therefore, when you open a jar of sott'olio, be careful: if the lid is domed up, and there's a whisper of air escaping the jar, discard it, because it may not be safe.

2 medium eggplants

1 lb. 2 oz. zucchini

2 cups water

salt

¾ cup white wine vinegar
(see page 112)

5 or 6 small garlic cloves, sliced

6 anchovy fillets, chopped (optional)

1 teaspoon dried chili flakes

1 teaspoon dried oregano

6 fresh mint leaves, roughly chopped

extra-virgin olive oil, for covering

Equipment needed

large strainer

some kind of heavy weight

2 warm, dry sterilized 1-pt. glass jars
(see page 114)

Makes 2 x 1 pint jars

1 Start by removing some of the eggplant skin with a vegetable peeler, creating stripes. I personally like leaving some of the skin on for the chewy texture and great purple color, but it's up to you. Cut the eggplants into ¼ in. slices widthwise (they tend to hold their shape better the thicker they're cut). Salt each eggplant thoroughly, and layer in a large strainer with a heavy weight on top (anything heavy will work). The idea is to press out all of the bitter juices from the eggplants, leaving you with just the sweet flesh. Allow to drain for two hours until there is a pool of dark brown liquid below the strainer, then rinse and pat dry. Cut the zucchini lengthwise into ¼–⅜-in. slices.

2 In a medium-size saucepan, bring the water with some salt and 1 cup of the white wine vinegar to the boil. Add the sliced zucchini and cook for 4–5 minutes until tender, but still with a bite. Remove from the cooking liquid, reserving the liquid so you can repeat with the eggplant slices. They also take 4–5 minutes to cook and the eggplant will become bright and transparent when ready. It is better to do the eggplant last, as the vibrant purple color taints the cooking liquid.

3 Once both the zucchini and the eggplant are cooked and drained, you can just pat them dry with paper towels. Add the vegetables to the sterilized jars. You can do a jar of each, or mix them in layers.

4 All that is left to do is to make the dressing. Mix the garlic, anchovies, chili flakes, dried oregano, mint leaves, and remaining white wine vinegar with about 1 cup olive oil. Once it is mixed, pour it over the vegetable in the jars. If they are not completely covered, just fill up the jars with more olive oil. Tightly seal the jars (see page 114), and they are ready for use. They may be kept like this, refrigerated, for up to four weeks, so long as the olive oil level is kept so that the vegetables are covered. Keep in the bottom of the fridge, so the oil does not set, or just remove it from the fridge before you want to eat it, so that the oil becomes liquid again.

Making strawberry and vanilla jam

Let's face it, strawberry jam is a real classic. This fragile fruit isn't a great keeper, so for the best jam, capture the fruit at its freshest, preserving it in recognizable chunks. Here the strawberries have been teamed with vanilla, the perfect partner to make a truly delicious jam. This recipe uses slightly less sugar than a traditional strawberry jam might and consequently has a softer set, which means that if you are feeling really gluttonous, you can eat it straight from the jar. Swirl a few spoonfuls through a mixture of mascarpone and plain yogurt for a fast dessert, or dollop it onto a freshly baked biscuit—eating it quickly before the jam oozes away over the sides.

1 vanilla bean

9 cups strawberries, hulled
(larger fruits halved)

3⅜ cups sugar

juice of 3 lemons

Equipment needed

sugar thermometer

preserving pan

5 warm, dry sterilized ½-pt.
glass jars (see page 114)

Makes 4–5 cups

1 Split the vanilla bean lengthwise into four pieces and place in a bowl with the strawberries, tucking the bean pieces in among the fruit. Cover with the sugar and leave for 12 hours or overnight.

2 Pour the fruit, vanilla bean pieces, and juice into a preserving pan and add the lemon juice. Cook over low heat until the sugar has dissolved, stirring only now and then, so that the fruit stays intact. Turn up the heat and boil rapidly to reach setting point. Use a candy thermometer to test for this; it should read 220° F when placed in the center of the pan. Skim with a metal spoon if necessary to remove any scum, or stir in a small knob of butter to help it disperse.

3 Remove the vanilla bean pieces, scrape the seeds out of them, and add these to the jam, disposing of the beans. Stir the seeds through the jam.

4 Pour the jam into the jars. The jam can be stored for at least 12 months if kept unopened in a cool dark place.

Making ginger and lemon syrup

This syrup, though not intentionally medicinal, is soothing and warming and is ideal to drink as a hot beverage if you feel a cold coming on. Dilute it to taste with hot water.

2 lemons

piece of fresh gingerroot, about 5 x 1-in. (or equivalent in smaller pieces), bruised

5 cups water

sugar (for quantity, see step 2)

Equipment needed

clip-top or corked bottles or freezer containers

Makes about 3 cups

1 Juice and thinly pare the rind of the lemons. Put the ginger and lemon rind in a pan with the water. Simmer gently for 40 minutes.

2 Spoon out and discard the rind and ginger, then strain the liquid through a sieve into a measuring pitcher to remove any extra sediment. Add ¼ cup sugar to every ⅜ cup liquid and the lemon juice and stir over a low heat until all the sugar has dissolved. Bring just to the boil, then remove quickly from the heat.

3 Pour the syrup into clean clip-top or corked bottles and sterilize. To do so, place a folded cloth or trivet in a large pan and place the bottles on top. Pour in cold water to cover the bottles up to the neck, then bring to the boil and simmer for 20 minutes. Once cooled, the syrup will be ready to use. It will keep for several months if stored in a refrigerator. Alternatively, pour it into freezer containers, seal, and freeze. This will sterilize the syrup and keep it fresh for longer.

Using your produce

Quick vinegars

If you are short of time these two recipes will work perfectly well when making pickles and chutneys.

Pickling vinegar

1 quart cider or wine vinegar (see page 112) or malt vinegar

piece of fresh gingerroot, about 2 x 1 in., peeled and finely sliced

1 tablespoon each black peppercorns, mustard seeds, celery seeds

8 dried red chilies

2 teaspoons each whole allspice, whole cloves, coriander seeds

Makes 1 quart

1 Place all the ingredients on the top of a double boiler, over simmering water (or use a bowl over a saucepan.) Allow the vinegar to warm through without boiling, remove it from the heat, and leave the spices to steep in the warm vinegar for 2–3 hours.

2 Strain the spices from the vinegar before using.

Sweet pickling vinegar

2½ cups white wine vinegar (see page 112)

⅞ cup sugar

piece of fresh gingerroot ½-in. square

1 tablespoon each whole allspice, black peppercorns

Makes 2½ cups

1 Place the ingredients in a pan and stir over a low heat to dissolve the sugar.

2 Turn up the heat and boil for 1 minute, then remove from the heat. Strain the spices from the vinegar before using.

Onion marmalade

Serve an onion marmalade with pâté, cold meat, or sausages. If you like a contrast of textures, try mixing it with a mixture of onions, shallots, and even a few white pearl onions.

3 tablespoons extra-virgin olive oil

2 lb. onions, sliced

5 shallots, sliced

½ cup light muscovado, or good-quality brown, sugar

salt and freshly ground black pepper

3 tablespoons honey

1¼ cups red wine

⅓ cup cider vinegar, pasteurized (see page 112)

handful of raisins

Equipment needed

5 warm, dry sterilized ½-pt. glass jars (see page 114)

Makes about 5 cups

1 Heat the olive oil in a large skillet, and stir in the onions, shallots, and sugar. Season with salt and pepper. Cover the pan and cook over a gentle heat for 30 minutes, stirring occasionally with a wooden spoon.

2 Add the honey, wine, vinegar, and raisins. Continue cooking over a very low heat, still stirring from time to time, for about 20 minutes or until the onions make a thick syrup.

3 Remove from the heat immediately and pour into hot sterilized jars (see page 114). Seal in the usual way and leave to stand for at least 2–3 weeks before even trying it. Once you have opened the jar, keep it cool in the refrigerator and it will last for at least two months.

Beet chutney

If you grow beets in your garden, you may find, at the height of the season, that you've produced a surplus. This chutney (see also page 116) is a flavorful way of using them up.

2 lb. raw beets, peeled and coarsely grated
1 lb. onions, peeled and chopped
1½ lb. cooking apples, peeled, cored, and chopped
3 cups seedless raisins
1 quart pickling vinegar (see page 124)
4 cups sugar
2 teaspoons ground ginger

Equipment needed
stainless steel preserving pan
9 warm, dry sterilized ½-pt. glass jars (see page 114)

Makes about 9 cups

1 Place everything in a stainless steel preserving pan and stir over a gentle heat to dissolve the sugar. Bring to the boil, then simmer gently for about 1 hour until the beets and onions are soft and the chutney is thick but still juicy, stirring occasionally.

2 Pour the chutney into the jars and seal. Once opened, keep in the refrigerator and it should keep for several months.

Piccalilli

The Edwardians were very fond of chutneys and pickles, which were often eaten with a cold collation of beef, tongue, or ham.

1 lb. green tomatoes, sliced

1 lb. green beans, sliced

1 lb. carrots, sliced

1 cauliflower, cut into florets

1 lb. pickling onions, peeled

½ (rounded) cup salt

7½ pints water

3 rounded tablespoons mustard powder

3 rounded tablespoons ground ginger

1 rounded tablespoon ground turmeric

1 teaspoon celery seeds

½ cup sugar

1 quart white wine vinegar, pasteurized (see page 112)

¼ cup cornstarch

Equipment needed

warm, dry sterilized glass jars (see page 114)

Makes 6–7 cups

1 Put the vegetables into a large bowl and add the salt and water. Stir thoroughly and weight the vegetables so they are immersed in the water.

2 Heat the spices, sugar, and most of the vinegar in a saucepan, and simmer, stirring occasionally, for about 5 minutes.

3 Rinse the vegetables and add them to the pan. Bring to the boil and simmer for about 15 minutes or until they are soft but still a little crunchy. Strain the vegetables, reserving the cooking liquid, and pack them quite tightly into warm sterilized jars.

4 Stir the cornstarch into the remaining vinegar and add it to the cooking liquid. Bring to the boil and cook for a few minutes, stirring constantly until it has thickened.

5 Pour over the vegetables in the jars, leave to cool, and then seal (see page 114.) Keep it in a cool for at least 6 weeks before eating to allow the flavors to mellow.

Pickled shallots

Pickled onions are a favorite relish in Britain, where they often form part of the traditional "plowman's lunch," accompanying a wedge of sharp cheese and some crusty bread and butter. Pearl onions are normally used, but shallots, with their sweeter flavor, make an interesting alternative. To be sure that your shallots retain that initial crunch, they need to be marinated in brine for a few days before being packed into jars and covered in spiced vinegar. Besides that, this pickle must be the easiest there is, and you should always keep a few jars on the pantry shelf.

2 lb. small, rounded shallots

⅝ cup salt

2½ cups pickling vinegar (see page 124)

Equipment needed

6 warm, dry sterilized ½-pt. glass jars (see page 114)

Makes 6 cups

1 Place the shallots in a large bowl without skinning them. Make the brine by dissolving half of the salt in water, then pour this over the shallots and leave in a cool dark place for 12 hours. Drain and skin the shallots.

2 Make up a second batch of brine using the remaining salt and the same amount of water, pour it over the shallots, and leave for another 2–3 days.

3 Drain and rinse the salt from the onions and pack them tightly into sterilized jars. Pour the pickling vinegar over them so that they are completely covered. Cover and seal the jars (see page 114.) The shallots will keep their flavor and crispness for up to six months after bottling.

Cherry jam

You can use a black cooking cherry, such as a Morello cherry, for this jam, or a lighter eating cherry (reduce the sugar to taste for these,) and the color of your jam will vary accordingly. Note that, unlike the strawberry and vanilla jam (see page 120), here the fruit is cooked before the sugar is added. If you grow your own cherries (or strawberries, for that matter,) make sure to pick them as soon as they ripen, or else the birds will eat all of them before you get the chance. As with all jams, the jars should be sterilized before use.

5–6 cups cherries (about 1½ lb.)
2¼ cups sugar
1 tablespoon lemon juice

Equipment needed
cherry stoner
preserving pan
3 sterilized ½-pt. jars (see page 114)

Makes approx. 3 cups

1 Pit the cherries using a cherry stoner over a basin to catch any juice. Place the stones in a piece of muslin and tie it into a bag with string. Put the fruit and juice into a pan with 2 tablespoons water and simmer gently until the fruit is just cooked.

2 Warm the sugar in a bowl in the oven on its lowest setting for around 20 minutes. Add the sugar and the lemon juice to the fruit and stir over a low heat until all the sugar has dissolved, then turn up the heat and.boil rapidly to reach setting point. Remove the muslin bag and leave the jam for 5–10 minutes, then stir to redistribute the cherries. Skim if necessary.

3 Pour the jam into the jars and seal. It should keep for at least six months if kept, unopened, in a cool, dark place.

Plum and pear jam

Unlike the strawberries in the jam on page 120, ripe plums are full of natural sugar and pectin, so they can be used in one of the few jam recipes that need absolutely no added sugar. You must, of course, use very soft, ripe plums and pears in this recipe to achieve the right sweetness and set. It is therefore an ideal way of coping with windfalls, provided you cut out any bruises or damage from the fruit. This recipe is more like a purée than a true jam in texture, but it will keep for months, provided you store it in the refrigerator.

2 lb. ripe eating plums, stoned and halved
zest and juice of 1 orange
stick of cinnamon, crushed
2 cloves
8 cups water
2 lb. pears, peeled, cored and roughly chopped
zest and juice of 1 lemon
2 tablespoons honeyed sweet dessert wine (optional)

Equipment needed
preserving pan
5 or 6 sterilized ½-pt. jars (see page 114)

Makes 4½–6 cups

1 Put the plums in a preserving pan with the orange juice and zest, the cinnamon, cloves, and water over low heat and simmer for about 20 minutes, stirring frequently, or until the fruit is fairly soft.

2 Add the pears, along with the lemon zest and juice and sweet wine, if using. Simmer, stirring occasionally, for another hour, or until the fruit has reduced to a thick pulp. Add more water if necessary at any time to prevent the fruit from sticking to the bottom of the pan.

3 If you like jam very smooth and more like a purée, pass it through a sieve; otherwise bottle it as it is in warm, dry sterilized jars. Leave it to cool before sealing the jars and store in a cool place. The jam will keep for at least six months if unopened.

Elderflower syrup

The shrubby elder (*Sambucus nigra*) is so common in some parts of the United States that it is easy to pass by. Yet in early summer it provides one of the most distinctive ingredients of the preserving year. The heavily scented blossoms make a refreshing syrup (made following a similar method to that for the ginger and lemon syrup on page 122), which you can dilute with still or sparkling mineral water. The fragrance, as well as the taste, evokes lazy summer afternoons. Gather the flower heads on dry, sunny days, away from busy roads, and select those that are fresh and white, avoiding older creamy-yellow blossoms.

20 heads of elderflower

6½ cups sugar

5 cups water

3 tablespoons citric acid

2 lemons, thinly sliced

2 oranges, thinly sliced

Equipment needed

clip-top or corked bottles

Makes about 3 pints

1 Shake the flowers, face down, to remove any unwanted insects.

2 Place the sugar and water in a stainless steel or enamel pan and warm slowly, stirring, to dissolve the sugar completely, then bring the resulting syrup to a boil.

3 Add the flowers, return to the boil, then remove from the heat.

4 Add the other ingredients, stir well, then leave, covered, in a cool place for 24 hours.

5 Strain the cooled syrup into clean clip-top or corked bottles and sterilize (see page 114.)

6 This delicious syrup will keep for around 2 months in the refrigerator; if frozen in plastic containers, it will last for a year or more—so be sure to make plenty.

Chapter 5

THE BUTCHER'S

Meat has long been a much-valued part of our diet, and the profession of the butcher is an ancient one that can be traced back to the medieval guilds. For generations, the butcher's shop, with its display of cuts of meat, poultry, sausages, and hams, was an important establishment among a town or city's shops. Nowadays, the butcher's shop is all too often something of an endangered breed, so if you have a good butcher's nearby, do support it.

A good butcher sources their meat carefully, ideally visiting the farms from which the meat comes from to see how the livestock is reared. Other than the issue of animal welfare, there is a practical reason for this focus on the producer, since well-reared animals, such as grass-fed cattle or free-range chickens, produce good meat. A good butcher will also be able to cut up the animals into the various different joints of meat, though these days many butchers simply buy in pre-packed, ready-jointed cuts.

For hundreds of years, meat was a luxury, enjoyed by the wealthy and privileged, with the ability to dine on good meat a sign of high social status in many cultures. This precious, protein-rich food was not to be wasted, and many of the traditional foods made from meat—especially in Europe—are ingenious ways of using up every scrap of an animal carcass: blood sausages; parcels based on variety meats, such as haggis and faggots; and brawn, made from the pig's head.

Pigs

Of all the livestock used for meat, the pig is the animal that yields most varied types of meat products, such as bacon, lardons, hams, pancetta, sausages, salami, and chorizo. Thought to have been domesticated from the wild pig in 7,000 B.C.E., the pig was valued for its ability to forage for food and thrive on scraps, becoming in the process a large creature, which represented valuable eating. Its fat has also been valued historically for its flavor and for the succulence it gave to products such as sausages and salamis, although modern breeds of pigs are bred to be leaner than traditional ones. Pork fat was also rendered down to make lard, used in potting (see page 140) and pastry. There is a venerable tradition of "nose to tail" eating of pigs, with every part of the slaughtered animal used in a range of ingenious ways. In France, a huge and varied range of products made from pork is at the center of the country's charcuterie tradition.

Cows

Beef is another popular meat, with the carcass producing a range of cuts, from cheap ones, such as fat-rich ox cheeks or oxtail, ideal for slow-braising, to highly regarded, prestigious cuts, such as tender, lean fillet steak and rib of beef. Veal is the term given to the meat from calves, highly esteemed in France and Italy. The best beef comes from grass-fed cattle, rather than cattle that have been intensively reared indoors on a diet of grain, with well-marbled beef—in which the fat is spread out through the meat—a good indicator of quality. Breeds of cattle that are bred for beef include the Charolais, Hereford, and Aberdeen Angus.

Sheep

Another domesticated source of meat is the sheep, from which we get both lamb and mutton—the term given to meat from sheep over one year old. In some countries, lamb is eaten very young indeed, still at the suckling stage, but it is more more usually eaten when weaned, between 4 months and a year.

Poultry

Due to intensive farming, chicken—once a luxury—is now an everyday staple, with chicken breast fillet a hugely popular cut. Free-range chickens, with access to an outdoor space where they can forage for food, have both more texture and flavor than mass-produced, battery-farmed chickens, where both movement and the chance to express natural behavior are restricted. Other poultry include the turkey, which, due to its large size, is a popular choice for festive meals such as Thanksgiving dinner; the duck, with its fat-rich flesh; and the goose, appreciated for its distinctive, rich flavor.

Game

Game—the term applied to wild animals caught through hunting—is a traditional food in many countries, now often regarded as a luxury. Game, such as wild boar, wild deer, grouse, and wild ducks, are noted for their flavor and the leanness of their meat—a result of their active outdoor lives.

Preserving meat

Good butchers "hang" their meat: a process of dry-aging the meat in a carefully controlled, cool, well-ventilated environment. The enzyme action in this process both tenderizes the meat and gives it flavor. Drying meat is thought to be the most ancient form of preserving meat, a tradition still represented today in products such as biltong (South African cured beef.)

Salting is another long-practiced way of preserving meat by removing moisture, since salt has a dehydrating effect. Human beings have long valued salt for its flavor and for its preserving qualities, both mining it from the ground and producing it by evaporating seawater. The role of salt as a preservative is explored further in the next chapter. Many of our air-dried meats were traditionally made through complex, time-consuming processes, which both used salt and encouraged the process of fermentation within the meat to make an environment in which bacteria cannot survive. Today, many preserved meat products are enjoyed in their own right as luxuries, such as meltingly soft rillettes and the

confit of duck used to add flavor and succulence to a French cassoulet. The industrialization of meat product manufacture, however, has seen many shortcuts taken to speed up traditional processes, such as the addition of "improvers" like glucono delta lactone (GDL), an acidifying agent, to create salamis in a few hours, rather than several weeks. The difference in flavor between a lovingly cured meat product, produced with skill and time, and a mass-produced product, where technology and additives have been used to bypass the traditional process, is noticeable. Although these crafts are threatened, there are still skilled butchers and artisanal producers committed to creating fine meat products. The home cook looking to work with meat has many options open to explore, from making sausages and potting meats to slow-cooking pâtés and terrines.

Sausages

Originating from the frugal desire to make use of every precious scrap of meat, the sausage, usually defined as a mixture of finely chopped or ground seasoned meat in a casing, exists in many forms. Although pork is a popular choice of meat for sausages, they can be made from any meat, including beef, lamb, venison, and also poultry, such as duck or chicken.

Sausages trace their history to antiquity, with the word "sausage" having its roots in the Latin *salsus*, meaning "salted." Traditionally, the casings for the chopped meat were made from animal's intestines, used as a natural container for the meat filling, with the long, narrow shape that characterizes a classic sausage shape deriving from the shape of the casing.

Another natural wrapping for sausages is caul fat (the lacy, fatty membrane that encases the internal organs), which is used to wrap around sausage meat patties such as Greece's sheftalia. Although artificial casings (usually from collagen) are now widely used in the mass-manufacture of sausages, natural or "fresh" casings made from animal intestines are still used today. They are preferred by artisanal sausage makers, who value their slightly porous quality, which allows the sausages to dry gradually and to cook without bursting.

Broadly speaking, sausages can be divided into the following different groups:

Fresh sausages Made from fresh meat, these are raw and perishable. They must be cooked before eating and should be consumed within a few days of making.

Cured sausages Dried, salted sausages, which can be sliced and eaten without cooking, such as Italy's salami crudo and France's saucisson sec. In the Mediterranean region—France, Italy, Greece, and Spain—the dry, warm climate enables curing to take place easily, and there is a long tradition of making this type of spiced, dry, salty, cured sausage.

Cooked or part-cooked sausages These are sausages that are cooked or part-cooked during production. North European countries, such as Poland and Germany, with their cold, wet climates, have a long tradition of making cooked sausages, many of which are also smoked to enhance their flavor and keeping properties.

Left: Paprika gives chorizo sausage its distinctive red coloring
Opposite: Parma ham and salami for sale at Lidgate's

Meet the producer: Lidgate's

A much-respected, well-established butcher's, Lidgate's is a family affair, currently run by David Lidgate, the fourth generation of the family to manage the business. All their meat is meticulously sourced from free-range and organic farms and carefully selected with an eye to quality.

"I vet all the meat that comes into the shop," explains David, "and if I don't think it's good enough, I'll send it back. I know by the look and the feel of the carcass whether it's what I want. It's like tasting a wine in a restaurant before you buy it." This careful sourcing means that their smart shop offers an eye-catching display of meat and meat products, from salt marsh lamb and grass-fed beef to Lidgate's famous savory pies and home-cured hams and salamis.

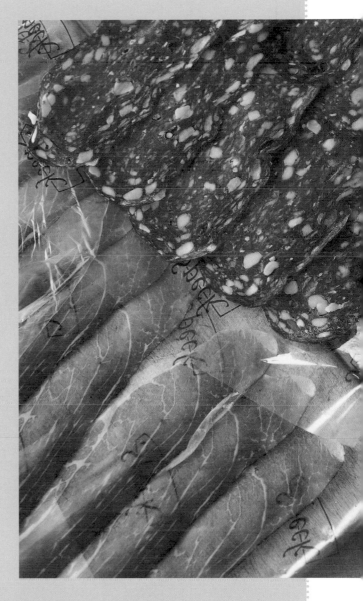

Among the bestsellers are their sausages, freshly made by Lidgate's every morning. For David, the quality of the meat he uses is key. "You can't make a good sausage without good pork," he declares, "and by that I mean pork from properly reared, properly fed pigs. All our pork comes from pigs grown in the open air, with access to fields. Some producers are using woodlands to feed their pigs, which is great. The pigs love acorns and beech mast, and it not only gives a slightly nutty flavor, but also makes for healthy pigs. Happy pigs make good pork.

"It's not just the quality of our meat that's important to our sausages, it's the quality of everything else that goes in them. Our herbs and spices have to be fresh, because if they're old and stale, they'll lack flavor. Although our sausages are lean, we don't make the leanest sausages because you need some fat in the recipe to give the sausage flavor and succulence. We use around 15–20 percent of fat, but it must be good fat. I can tell whether the fat is good or not by its color and feel. We use natural casings because I think they produce a better product. The artificial casings dry out more, especially where the linkage is, and that looks unattractive. Our sausages are displayed loose—not packeted—and they must look good as well as taste good. We taste everything we make, from the pies to our hams. It's not rocket science; it's hard work and liking what you do."

Fresh sausages

Classically, makers of fresh sausages use a mixture of lean meat and fat to make the filling, with the fat needed to give succulence and flavor. An often recommended ratio of lean to fat is three to four parts lean to one part fat, though sausage makers may well tweak this ratio in their own personal recipe. In Western Europe and North America, pork, with its natural high fat content, is the favored meat for sausage making, whether fresh, cured, or cooked. This meat mixture can then be flavored in many ways, traditionally with herbs such as sage, flavorings such as garlic, or spices such as the sweet or hot paprika used in Spanish chorizo. Whereas a craft butcher will make his own sausages with a high meat content using a mixture of fat and lean meat, such as shoulder and leg, low-grade sausages are made with a low proportion of meat, bulking out the sausages with rusk, bread, and water. In addition, the meat content used will be mechanically recovered meat (MRM), which forms a pulpy mass. The joy of making your own sausages is, of course, that you are in control of what goes into them.

To make sausages, the meat mixture is first ground to create sausage meat, a process usually done using a grinder or a food processor. Because the grinding process heats up the meat, it is recommended that you work with very cold meat. The texture of the ground sausage meat can be varied to personal taste, with a very fine grind producing a smooth sausage and a rougher, coarser-cut grind producing a more textured one. This meat mixture is then seasoned to taste with spices, herbs, and other flavorings. In order to check that you have achieved the right level of seasoning, fry a little piece of the sausage meat mixture until cooked through and sample it to check that the flavoring is as you want it. Making sausages in small batches allows you to flavor them well and evenly.

Cured sausages

The process of making dry-cured sausages is a more time-consuming one. As with fresh sausages, the meat mixture should contain a proportion of fat, usually in a ratio of one part fat to two or three parts lean meat, to ensure succulence. Hard pork back fat is often favored because of its firm texture. The meat is finely diced, ground, or pounded to a paste. Differences in the texture of the meat mixture are used to create different types of dry-cured sausages; for example, France's saucisson de montagne is made with more coarsely ground meat than saucisson de ménage.

The dry-curing process requires dehydration, and so salt is added to the meat to draw out the water from it. A tiny amount of nitrite is also added to inhibit bacterial growth and give the cured meat a red color rather than the grey color naturally produced by the process. In addition, spices and flavorings are added, such as peppercorns in Felino salami, and sometimes alcohol, such as red wine. The mixture is tightly packed into the casings to make sure that there are no pockets of air in which bacteria could thrive, then set aside to dry out for several weeks, usually in a cool, well-ventilated place. Natural casings are favored for dry-cured sausages, as they act as a protective barrier, but allow the meat to "breathe" and gradually dehydrate. As the sausages dry, they develop a harmless white mold bloom on their surface, an indicator that the maturing is progressing as it should. During the maturing of many types of dry-cured sausages, the lactic-acid bacteria present in the meat set to work, partly fermenting it. This acidic environment, in which bacteria find it hard to exist, then extends these sausages' keeping qualities. The maturing process results in aromatic, intensely flavored sausages with a firm texture.

Cooked or part-cooked sausages

When it comes to cooked sausages, parboiling, boiling, and smoking are all ways of cooking them. Italy's large, fine-textured mortadella sausage, made from pork flavored with peppercorns and pistachios, is steamed or poached. German bratwurst sausages are scalded during the making process and should then be heated before eating. Smoking, which adds a distinctive flavor, is often combined with other processes, such as dry-curing or parboiling.

Opposite: A selection of salami

Hams

Strictly speaking, a ham is the cured back leg of an animal, although the term is often used to include the cured shoulder. Most people think of a ham as coming from a pig, but it can also be used to describe meats such as mutton and venison.

There are many different types of hams, with recipes varying not only from country to country, but also from region to region. England's Bradenham ham, for example is dry cured, then soaked in a brine flavored with molasses and finally smoked, resulting in a subtle, sweet-flavored ham, whereas Wiltshire ham is cured in brine. Virginia-style ham is dry-cured and typically hickory smoked. Many of the finest hams, such as Italy's Parma ham or Spain's Iberico ham, are dry-cured hams, produced by an intricate process of salting the meat and setting it aside to cure in cool, airy conditions for many months. The true Iberico ham is made from a specific breed of pig, Spain's indigenous Iberico (also known as pata negra or the "black-hoofed" pig), with the best ham coming from pigs which forage for acorns and wild plants in forests. The resulting hams are costly luxuries with a rich, distinctive flavor and texture, classically simply sliced and eaten.

Above: Ham going through the air-drying process

Meet the producer: Trealy Farm

Trealy Farm, in Wales, is noted for its range of around 50 fresh and charcuterie pork products, all carefully produced on the farm itself.

"Our starting point is that we use locally sourced, free-range, traditional breeds of pigs," declares owner James Swift. "These are slow-growing breeds that have denser, drier meat ideal for charcuterie. These traditional breeds also produce more marbled meat, which you want, as you need the fat for flavor, moisture, and texture. We want pigs that weigh about 100kg [220 lb.], at which point they're up to a year old.

"These pigs are then seam butchered—that is, cut by muscle, so every muscle is taken out. From each muscle we make at least one, sometimes two or three, products," explains James. "Different muscles have different qualities. Silverside, for example, is a muscle

that does a lot of work, so it's tough. We use that for a Monmouthshire air-dried ham. Chump, another muscle at the end of the loin, is very tender. We use that to make a beech-smoked, air-dried ham, which is much softer and more delicate than the Monmouthshire."

The process of transforming this pork into sausages and charcuterie is "very scientific." "All our air-dried products are naturally fermented, and to do that we need to control the environment every step of the way. Very small differences in the process will affect the flavor." The type of salt used to dry-cure his products is very important. "Salts vary in their flavors and action, so you'll find charcuterie producers always source their salt from one particular area or producer; we're currently experimenting with sea salt from Anglesea. We also need nitrites to prevent botulism, so we use organic curing salts with a very low nitrite content, about a fifth of what you'd normally get."

James is committed to creating charcuterie products using traditional, time-consuming methods. "We don't use monosodium glutamate (MSG), as lots of people do. We want to work with natural flavors, so to use MSG seems a bit of a cheat." The curing period for Trealy Farm's products can be up to 5–6 months for the hams. "Because we're curing muscles rather than legs, they're smaller pieces of meat, so they don't take so long." The result of his careful sourcing of the meat and intricate process of curing is an individual range of subtly flavorful charcuterie. For James, it is the fact that he is producing something unique that places him in the great tradition of charcuterie. "People talk about air-dried ham as though it's one thing, but it's not. There are hundreds of different hams or different chorizos, all of which can vary enormously from each other, depending on how they're made, the breed of pig, the microclimate where they're produced. To me, that's the beauty of charcuterie."

Pâtés and terrines

Pâtés and terrines are a family of products made from finely ground meat, poultry, or fish. French cuisine is especially noted for its wide range. The term "terrine" comes from the French name for a type of lidded, ovenproof dish in which pâtés are cooked, and is generally taken to imply pâté with a relatively chunky texture, often layered.

Classic ingredients for both pâtés and terrines include variety meats, such as liver, and game, which is valued for its strong taste. Popular flavorings include onion, garlic, herbs, spices, and—a luxurious touch—truffles. The mixture is gently baked, sometimes in a bain-marie, and served hot or cold. A soft, melting, or delicate texture is characteristic of pâtés and terrines, which are usually served with bread or crackers.

Potted meat and fish

A traditional way of preserving meat or fish is to coat it with a layer of fat, such as clarified butter, to keep out the air. Known as "potting," this process is no longer much practiced in the U.S., although it remains popular in Britain.

In European cookery it traces its history to medieval pie-making, where the pastry case was used as a way of sealing and keeping the edible contents. Spices, such as nutmeg or mace, are usually added during the process for flavor. The preserving properties of this process can be extended by first salting the meat before coating it in fat and also by long,

slow cooking to draw out the moisture from the meat. This extended process is used in France to make what is known as confit, in which a piece of meat or poultry is first salted, then soaked in brine, then cooked very slowly and gently in fat until the meat is cooked through. Classically, the fat should come from the meat being preserved; hence, pork, goose, or duck, all rich in fat, are the preferred meats for the confit process. The dish is then set aside, with the liquid fat hardening over the meat and providing a protective coating; it is very important that the meat be covered completely by the fat to prevent decay. Sealed, usually in stoneware pots or cans, the confit can be kept safely for months. Another French charcuterie product based on potting is rillettes, made by

Meet the producer: Baxters Potted Shrimps

Established in 1799, this tiny Lancashire company, still run by the Baxter family, has a proud history of producing potted shrimp, with a Royal Warrant from Her Majesty The Queen as a distinguished sign of approval. With a subtle taste of, at a guess, mace and nutmeg, these pots are a lovingly produced delicacy.

"We use locally caught little brown shrimps," explains Mark Smith, manager of Baxters. "That's very important, as this stretch of the northwest coast produces a very good quality of shrimp; the reason they're so good is in the handling. The guys we buy the shrimps from are third and fourth generation fisherman; all they've done is fish for shrimp. They go out in small boats with a net, pull the net in, then they go riddling through the catch, that's what they call it, picking through and grading the shrimps by size. They boil the shrimps in seawater on board the fishing boat, then place them in a net and put them in the sea over the side of the boat to cool them. This is the same way they've done it for hundreds of years. They then shell the shrimps, which is really laborious, but hand peeling, rather than using machines to peel them, results in shrimps with more flavor.

"These are the shrimps that we buy. We then pick through the shrimps ourselves, picking out any tiny bits of shell that are left. I cook 30 lb. of peeled shrimps at a time. We call it a 'stewing,' where we cook them with spices and butter. The spice mixture we use is a family secret, handed down through the generations. I can tell you that we don't use clarified butter; we use the best English butter, the same we've used for years. Once cooked, the shrimps are cooled, chilled, then placed in pots. We use very little butter in our final product; our potted shrimps are 85% shrimp, 15% butter. We put a very thin layer of butter on top to seal them and give them a better shelf life.

"The way we produce our potted shrimps is still the same as it has been all through the years; there's no difference in flavor between what we make now and what we made 50 years ago. Like a good cheese, potted shrimps are best eaten at room temperature when the butter has softened. First you get the small, sweet, tender, moist shrimps, then the tongue-tingling aftertaste of the spices. There are a lot more people making potted shrimps nowadays, but ours are still the best."

cooking meat (traditionally pork or goose) extremely slowly in fat until tender, then shredding, pounding, or mashing the meat, placing it in containers, and topping with a layer of fat. Fish rillettes are often made with oily fish, such as eel, salmon, or sardine, again cooked very gently in butter, then pounded into a paste. Although these dishes originated in the need to preserve food, they are now considered very much as indulgent luxuries, valued for their rich, melting texture and depth of flavor.

Opposite: A freshley baked baguette is the perfect accompaniment to any pâté or terrine
Right: When making potted meat or fish, add some herbs and peppercorns to the hot butter to increase the depth of flavor

Sourcing the ingredients

Try to source your meat carefully from a reputable source, such as a good butcher's or a farm shop. Meat from slow-reared pigs killed when they are older is better for charcuterie purposes, because it is drier, rather than wet meat from pigs killed at just a few months' old. Modern breeds of pig have been bred to have leaner meat than was traditional, to gain weight fast, and to have long bodies. Traditional breeds (now known as rare breeds) of pig are hardy creatures, adept at foraging outdoors, which gain weight slowly, so making for marbled meat and a good outer layer of fat. Meat from traditional breeds of pig, reared with access to the outdoors so that they can forage, not only is more flavorful but also has the level of fat needed to produce good charcuterie.

Salt plays a major part in curing meats. For a look at different types of salt, please see page 166. Sodium nitrite, which is needed to guard against the risk of botulism, can be hard to get hold of. However, special preserving salts containing sodium nitrite are available to the public, and a quick search online will bring up several specialist mail-order companies.

Natural sausage casings are often recommended for their porous quality. These can be sourced online or via reputable butchers. Before use, natural casings need to be soaked for at least two hours, ideally overnight. For caul fat—also called lace fat—which is used to wrap around meat parcels, you also need to find a good butcher; it is relatively expensive.

How to store

Always store your meat and meat products carefully, and eat them within the recommended period of consumption. Fresh sausages, for example, should be kept in the refrigerator and eaten within a day or two. If they won't be consumed soon, it is best to freeze them, then thaw as required.

While whole dried salamis are a preserved product that can be stored in a cool, dry, well-ventilated place, the reality of centrally heated well-insulated homes means that it's safer to store them in a refrigerator, loosely wrapped in breathable wrapping. Be sure to keep products designed to be eaten raw, such as salamis, well away from fresh meat, poultr, or fish to avoid any risk of cross-contamination.

Left: Salami lightly spiced with fennel seeds
Right: The white coating often found on the outside of salami is mold, which helps to protect it from outside elements

Making chorizo sausages

These Spanish-style sausages pack a great tasty kick. Ideally, make them a day ahead to allow the flavors really to meld and permeate. The most important thing to think about for this recipe is the hygiene factor in making ground meat products. You must remember that all the bacteria on the outside of the pork are going to be mixed up into the finished sausage meat, so make sure that everything you are going to use is clean and the work surfaces are sterilized. Just follow your normal good practices of washing hands and cleaning up as you go. When you first start, you can ask your local butcher to help with the casings and the meat. If you want to go on and experiment with many different sausages, you might like to try more specialized equipment and ingredients.

6 feet sausage casing

2 lb. pork loin

2 lb. fresh side pork

2 tablespoons coarse sea salt

5 garlic cloves, minced

2 tablespoons paprika

2 teaspoons cayenne pepper

1 teaspoon ground cumin

1 teaspoon dried oregano

¼ scant cup dry Spanish wine

Equipment needed

food mixer with a grinder and sausage-making attachment

large mixing bowl

Makes 4½ lb.

Note: When you first start to make sausages at home, you will need only the equipment listed above. However, if you are making more than a few pounds at a time, you might consider buying an electric meat grinder with sausage attachments. Alternatively, you can buy your meat already ground.

1 Soak your casings in plenty of cold water for a minimum of 2 hours to soften them and to remove the excess salt. Wash them again after soaking. Wash the insides of the casings by running water through them, then load onto the tube just before you need them.

2 Make sure that your butcher has trimmed all the rind off the pork. Weigh out the seasonings and meaure out the wine, so you are ready to get started as soon as the meat is ready (see step 3).

3 Cut the meat into small chunks about 1-in. square, so it will go through the grinder easily. Cover and place the meat in the refrigerator or freezer for no more than an hour, possibly less. You need the meat to be as near to frozen as possible, but DO NOT actually freeze it, or the texture will be like sawdust in the sausage. Put the meat through the grinder using a coarse grinder plate, collecting it in a bowl.

4 Add all the other ingredients and mix well. You will feel the meat start to firm up as you mix it. The more you mix, the firmer the texture will be in the finished sausage, so test-cook small pieces as you go until you find the consistency that suits you. At this stage, you can re-grind with a small-holed plate if you want a finer sausage, or leave it coarse, depending on the texture you desire.

5 Change the grinder plate to a sausage filling tube, load on the washed casings and force the meat back through the grinder to fill the skins. Tie a knot at the free end of the sausage casing. Hold the casing between your thumb and forefinger and push the filling down with the plunger. You will need to work by trial and error to get the correct pressure needed to fill the casings and the speed of moving your hand away from the tube. Use your free hand to twist the casings as they reach the desired length. Four or five twists between links are all that are needed. At first you may find they are too thick and can burst, or they may be too thin; but with practice your sausages will come good. The other thing you may find is that you get air pockets forming in the sausages as a result of not filling the hopper with enough meat. Try to get everything working evenly; speed is not important at this stage. Also, get someone to help the first time you make sausages, as it definitely does make it easier.

6 Wrap the links in baking parchment and leave in the fridge overnight so that the flavors have time to combine and develop. You can then cook them, or cut into individual links and store in the refrigerator for up to three days, or freeze them.

MAKING CHORIZO SAUSAGES **145**

Making game terrine

A game terrine such as this should be made two or three days in advance, so the flavors have plenty of time to mellow and blend. It needs a mixture of game meat along with pork and pork fat for flavor, moisture, and texture. You can make this recipe with venison, rabbit, or—if you can find it—wild boar.

1 lb. game meat, such as venison, stripped off the bone

¼ lb. ham, diced

¼ lb. pork fat, diced

½ teaspoon allspice

pinch of cloves

pinch of nutmeg

3½ tablespoons brandy

3½ tablespoons Madeira

salt and freshly ground pepper

1 lb. fresh side pork

1 egg

1 rounded tablespoon minced truffle (optional)

18 strips of bacon

Equipment needed

food processor

terrine dish

Serves 10–12

1 Cut half the venison (or other game) into finger-size strips. Mix the strips in a bowl with the ham, pork fat, allspice, cloves, and nutmeg. Pour in the brandy and Madeira, season, and stir thoroughly. Cover the bowl and leave to marinate for 1–2 hours.

2 Preheat the oven to 350°F. Put the remaining venison, along with the pork, in a food processor and blitz until reduced to pieces about 1-in. thick. Strain the liquid from the marinade into this mixture. Break in the egg, add the truffle (if using), salt, and pepper, and blitz again until reduced to pieces about half the previous size. (Be careful not to overprocess or chop it too finely, as this will result in a heavy and dense pâté.)

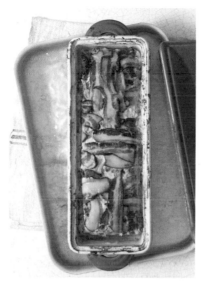

4 Place the terrine in a roasting pan and half fill the pan with boiling water. Bake in the preheated oven for 1¼–1½ hours. To test to see whether it is ready, remove the waxed paper and insert a skewer into the pâté: if the juices that run out are clear, it is cooked. Allow the terrine to cool slightly, then place a plate or a piece of wood on top and weight it with one or two small cans of food to press down the terrine. Refrigerate overnight and keep for at least 2 days before serving to allow the flavors to mellow. Keep the terrine well wrapped and refrigerated; it should last for up to five days.

3 Line a suitable terrine with the bacon, reserving two or three strips. Spread one-third of the chopped mixture on the bottom and cover with half of the venison mixture. Repeat the process and finish with a final layer of the chopped mixture. Cover the top with the remaining slices of bacon and lay a sheet of waxed paper on top.

Making bresaola

This classic Italian air-dried beef is very tasty indeed and well worth the slow nurturing process. Serve it finely sliced in an antipasto or as an appetizer by itself.

Aged until it becomes hard and turns a dark red, almost purple, color, bresaola can take up to three months to make, depending on the size of the beef you use. It is made from topside and is lean and tender with a sweet, musty smell.

This recipe has been adapted for home use, so I recommend using only 3 lb. of beef; this reduces the hanging time and thus the risk of spoiling. You also need to think about where you can hang your beef so that the temperature is just right at about 54°F.

2¾–3 lb. round steak
1 (rounded) tablespoon curing salt
⅛ (rounded) cup brown crystal sugar
1 teaspoon black pepper
½ cup fresh rosemary, chopped
½ cup fresh thyme, chopped
5 juniper berries

Equipment needed
pestle and mortar
plastic container
muslin
butcher's hook
Makes just over 1½ lb.

1 Trim the meat of all silverskin and external fat. Assemble all the cure ingredients, from the salt to the juniper berries.

2 Pound the cure ingredients in a mortar and pestle until fine. Rub half of the spice cure into the meat, making sure to cover it all, including the ends. Put in a plastic container, cover with plastic wrap, and refrigerate for 7 days, turning the meat every couple of days.

3 Drain any liquid that might be present and rub in the remaining spice cure. Cover with plastic wrap and refrigerate for another 7 days.

4 Take the meat from the refrigerator and rinse all the cure off thoroughly. Let it sit at room temperature for a couple of hours on a rack. Tie the whole thing up in a double layer of muslin and insert a butcher's hook into one end. Hang for at least a month at a temperature of about 54°F. When it is done, it will feel firm to touch, but still have a slight "give." As a guide, it should lose around 40 percent of its original weight. The bresaola will keep in the refrigerator for up to two weeks, in plastic wrap.

Making potted ham

This recipe is made using ham, but you can successfully substitute other cooked meat, such as leftover roast meat or poultry, so it is a useful way of using up scraps of meat that might otherwise be discarded.

1¾ sticks unsalted butter

1¼ cups roughly chopped,
good-quality cured ham,
fat removed

¼ teaspoon ground mace

½ teaspoon cayenne pepper

Equipment needed

food processor

4 ramekins or other small dishes

Serves 4

1 Preheat the oven to 300°F. First, clarify the butter. Simply place the butter in a heavy-based saucepan and heat very gently until the butter has totally melted. Skim off any white scum on the surface, then carefully spoon out the yellow clarified butter from the pan into a container, leaving behind the whitish residue of milky solids, which can be discarded. Place the ham in a food processor, together with two-thirds of the clarified butter, the mace, and the cayenne pepper. Blend until the mixture forms a fine-textured paste.

2 Divide the ham mixture evenly among the four ramekins and level the surface. Place the filled ramekins in a deep baking tray, pour in hot water so that it comes halfway up the sides of the ramekins, and bake for 20 minutes. Remove the ramekins from the oven and allow to cool. Once cool, use the remaining clarified butter to top each potted ham, forming a layer on top, and place in the refrigerator to chill. Before serving, bring the potted hams to room temperature to allow the butter to soften. The potted hams can either be stored in the refrigerator, where they will keep for a few days, or frozen.

Using your produce

Jambon persillé

This recipe is a variation of the terrine on page 146. If you buy the ham on the bone, allow extra for the weight of the bone and make sure you skin it before cooking. Jambon persillé should have quite a meaty—but not too overpowering—flavor, so it is a good idea to start off by boiling the joint, throwing away the water, and starting again. This way, you are certain of getting rid of some of the saltiness. If you do not have a terrine dish, you can make this in a bowl. The only disadvantage to this kind of terrine is that you will not be able to cut it into neat rectangular slices for serving, but if it tastes as good as it should, it is unlikely that your guests will mind.

1½ lb. smoked ham

11 black peppercorns

2 bay leaves

1 calf's foot

1 small knuckle of veal

few sprigs of chervil

few sprigs of tarragon

few sprigs of thyme

few sprigs of parsley

2 cups dry white wine

2 teaspoons white wine vinegar

large bunch of curly parsley, minced

Equipment needed

terrine or bowl

Serves 8

1 Put the ham in a deep saucepan, add just enough water to cover, and bring to the boil over medium heat. Just as the water starts to bubble, remove the pan from the heat, pour off the water, and start again. This time add 3 peppercorns and one of the bay leaves. Leave the ham to simmer gently for 25 minutes.

2 Lift the ham out of the water, and when it is cool enough to handle, trim away the fat and cut the meat into sizable chunks.

3 Meanwhile, in a clean saucepan, put the calf's foot, the knuckle of veal, the herbs tied together in a bunch, and the remaining bay leaf and peppercorns, along with about 4 cups of water. Bring to the boil over low heat, skimming off the fat as it rises. Cover and simmer gently for about 90 minutes, then pour in the wine, add the ham meat and simmer for another 30 minutes, or until the meat is very soft.

4 Using a slotted spoon, transfer the ham to a terrine or large bowl; flake it with a fork. Strain the liquid into a bowl through a strainer lined with muslin. Add the vinegar and leave it to set slightly, then stir in the parsley and pour it over the ham. Leave it overnight in a cold place to set. Serve it turned out on a serving dish and cut into slices. The dish will keep for three days in the refrigerator.

Parma ham with figs and balsamic dressing

The combination of sweet, salty Parma ham or a local prosciutto crudo—both air-dried meats, like bresaola (see page 149)—and a yielding soft fruit such as ripe figs or melon is one of life's little miracles. This is an all time classic, and none the worse for that. It is quick to assemble, provided you have excellent, thinly sliced ham and perfect, garnet-centered figs.

4 large or 8 small fresh ripe figs (preferably purple ones)

1 tablespoon good balsamic vinegar

extra-virgin olive oil

12 thin slices of Parma ham or prosciutto crudo

5 oz. fresh Parmesan cheese, broken into craggy lumps, to serve

crushed black pepper

Serves 4

1 Take each fig and stand it upright. Using a sharp knife, make two cuts across each fig, not quite quartering it, but keeping it intact. Ease the figs open and brush with balsamic vinegar and extra-virgin olive oil.

2 Arrange three slices of Parma ham on each plate and place the figs and Parmesan on top. Sprinkle with more oil and plenty of crushed black pepper.

Pork, fennel, and spinach terrine with drunken figs

I love the simplicity of this chunky terrine (see also page 146), made from pork, flavored with fennel seeds and layered with spinach. Its small size makes it perfect for a small party of guests or to serve for a simple snack or lunch.

2 bay leaves

8 strips dry-cured bacon

I cup chopped spinach

2 tablespoons olive oil

I small onion, chopped

I tablespoon fennel seeds

2 garlic cloves, minced

10 oz. fresh side pork, coarsely ground

½ lb. lean pork fillet, diced

½ teaspoon ground nutmeg

½ teaspoon ground allspice

I teaspoon coarse sea salt

½ teaspoon black pepper

slices of crusty bread, to serve

For the drunken figs

20 dried Turkish figs, halved

I cup Marsala wine

Equipment needed

small terrine or loaf tin oiled with canola oil

Serves 6

1 To make the drunken figs, put the figs, Marsala wine, and 4 tablespoons of water in a saucepan and bring nearly to boiling point. Remove from the heat, cover, and leave to cool.

2 Preheat the oven to 350°F. Place the bay leaves in the bottom of the terrine, then lay the bacon across the width. Put the spinach in a colander and pour boiling water over it to blanch. Refresh with cold water, squeeze out any excess water, and set aside.

3 Heat the olive oil in a skillet over low heat and sauté the onion, fennel seeds, and garlic for 10 minutes, or until soft but not yet brown. Transfer to a large bowl with half of the spinach, the side pork, and fillet, nutmeg, and allspice. Add the salt and pepper and mix well.

4 Put half of the pork mixture in the prepared terrine and press down firmly. Top with the spinach, then the remaining pork mixture. Press down firmly, then fold over any overhanging bacon. Firmly cover with oiled aluminum foil and put in a baking dish. Fill the baking dish with enough water to come halfway up the sides of the terrine. Bake in the oven for 1 hour. Transfer to a dish to catch any juices and put a weight on top. Leave to cool, then chill overnight or for 1–2 days. Serve with the drunken figs and bread. The terrine will keep for three days in the refrigerator.

Potted cheese

The potting process (see page 144) doesn't have to be restricted to meat; it can be used on other ingredients, too. Almost every traditional British cookbook includes at least one recipe for potted cheese, and there are hundreds of versions—with or without walnuts, anchovies, cayenne pepper, and even sometimes with a pinch of sugar. Here one of Mrs. Beeton's recipes has been adapted for modern-day machinery, as the food processor makes it unnecessary to pound by hand in a pestle and mortar as she did back in the mid-1800s.

½ lb. cheddar cheese
½ lb. (2 sticks) butter
large pinch of ground mace
large pinch of mustard powder
large pinch of cayenne pepper
3 tablespoons dry sherry

Equipment needed
food processor

Serves 4

1 Put all the ingredients in a food processor and blend until the mixture is smooth.

2 Spoon the mixture into an earthenware jar, cover with waxed paper, and store in a cool place. It will keep for several weeks, but is ready to be eaten within a couple of days.

Potted salmon

Properly done, potted fish is excellent (see also page 140). Don't be put off by the idea of fish paste, which is a corrupted form of potted fish—one of those extraordinary British inventions that, understandably enough, no other country has adopted with any enthusiasm.

½ lb. poached salmon, boned and cooled
3 anchovy fillets
juice of ½ lemon
2 sticks plus 3 tablespoons butter
pinch of mace
pinch of ground ginger
Salt and freshly ground black pepper

Serves 4

1 Pound the salmon with the anchovy fillets, lemon juice and 2 sticks of the butter until smooth (this is easier and quicker if done in a food processor). Add the mace and ginger and season to taste.

2 Pack the mixture tightly in a suitable pot. Melt the remaining butter and pour over the fish to seal. The salmon will keep in the refrigerator for up to 5 days.

Sausages with spinach, raisins, and pine nuts

Homemade sausages are perfect for this recipe, as there is absolutely no point in attempting it unless your pork sausages are meaty, luscious, and wrapped in natural skins.

1 tablespoon olive oil

10 good-quality pork sausages

2 large onions, finely sliced

2 garlic cloves, finely sliced

3 tablespoons balsamic vinegar

$\frac{1}{4}$ cup raisins

$\frac{1}{4}$ cup pine nuts

1 lb. fresh baby spinach, washed and drained

coarse sea salt and freshly ground pepper

mashed potatoes, to serve

Serves 3–4

1 Heat the oil in a large, heavy-based skillet, add the sausages, and fry gently for about 3–4 minutes or until the skins just begin to start browning all over. Toss in the onions and garlic and cook gently with the sausages until they begin to soften. Add the balsamic vinegar, raisins, and pine nuts and fry gently for a few minutes until the onions and pine nuts start to turn golden.

2 Pile the spinach on top of the sausages, turn down the heat, and, stirring constantly, wait until it has collapsed and wilted. Turn the heat up again and simmer until most of the liquid from the spinach has evaporated and the sauce is, once again, syrupy. Season and serve the sausages with the sauce spooned over a bowl of mashed potatoes.

Skinless sausages

Making your own sausages really is even easier when you avoid the time-consuming part of stuffing them into skins (see page 144). How, you are probably wondering, do they hold together? Very simply, the meat is chopped in a food processor, kneaded lightly with the hands, and rolled into sausage shapes, which are then wrapped in aluminum foil and lightly poached before being broiled or fried.

1 lb. lean fresh side or shoulder of pork

$\frac{1}{4}$ lb. fatback

1 garlic clove

bunch of flat-leaf parsley

large pinch of coarse sea salt

small pinch of ground cloves

small pinch of ground ginger

small pinch of ground nutmeg

$\frac{1}{2}$ cup fresh breadcrumbs

freshly ground black pepper

Equipment needed

food processor

foil and string

Makes 6 sausages

1 Roughly cut the pork and fat into pieces of a size that the food processor can handle. Put them in the food processor with the garlic, parsley, sea salt, cloves, ginger, nutmeg, breadcrumbs, and a generous amount of black pepper. Blitz until all the ingredients are mixed together and reduced to the texture of reasonably coarse breadcrumbs. You do not want to overprocess the meat, or this will make the sausage far too dense; on the other hand, if you do not process it enough, the mixture will not hold together.

2 Tip the meat out into a bowl and divide it into six equal portions. Using your fingers, knead the mixture lightly to make sure it sticks together, then roll it out between the palms into a sausage shape about 4 in. long. Wrap each sausage in a piece of foil and secure each end by twisting the foil tightly and tying it with string.

3 Have ready a large saucepan filled with gently simmering water. Drop in the sausages and simmer them for about 10 minutes. Using a slotted spoon, lift them out and put them in a colander. As soon as they are cool enough to handle, unwrap them and leave to drain.

4 Finish by browning them: either by brushing them lightly with olive oil and broiling them under a preheated broiler, or by frying them in a little olive oil or butter over moderate heat. Serve with onion marmalade or another chosen relish.

Smoky sausage and bean casserole

The Italians use a mixture of onions, carrots, and celery sautéed in olive oil as the base for many classic soups and casseroles. This "holy trinity" of veggies is called a soffritto and works well here in a hearty sausage stew.

1 tablespoon light olive oil

12 small sausages

1 garlic clove, chopped

1 leek, thinly sliced

1 carrot, diced

1 celery stalk, diced

2 cups chopped tomatoes

1 teaspoon Spanish smoked paprika

2 tablespoons maple syrup

2 sprigs of fresh thyme

2½ cups cannellini beans, drained and rinsed

toasted sourdough bread, to serve

Serves 4

1 Heat the oil in a heavy-based saucepan over high heat. Add the sausages in two batches and cook them for 4–5 minutes, turning often until cooked and an even brown all over. Remove from the pan and set aside.

2 Add the garlic, leek, carrot, and celery and cook for 5 minutes, stirring often. Add the tomatoes, paprika, maple syrup, thyme, beans, and 2 cups of water and return the sausages to the pan.

3 Bring to the boil, then reduce the heat to medium and simmer for 40–45 minutes, until the sauce has thickened.

4 Put a slice of toasted sourdough bread on each plate, spoon the casserole over the top, and serve.

Chapter 6

THE SMOKEHOUSE

Smoking food in order to enhance its keeping qualities is an ancient practice, the origins of which are lost in time. Certainly it is very easy to imagine that early hunters or fishermen seeking to dry their catch near a fire noticed the effect that the smoke had on the food, both flavoring it and causing it to stay safely edible for longer. The tradition of smoking food has been traced back to the Sumerians in Mesopotamia in 3,500 B.C.E., but is thought to have existed long before that. The ancient Greeks and Romans knew of smoking, using it as a way of preserving foods such as fish and cheese.

Early smoking

Although smoking can be done outside, over an open fire, it is simpler to smoke foods in an enclosed space. For much of human history, foods would have been smoked simply by hanging them in the chimney above the household hearth. However, given that smoking is both a smelly business and one, moreover, that carries the risk of fire, medieval Europe saw the construction of purpose-built smokehouses, traditionally narrow, high buildings in which the food could be placed above the smoke as it rose to the top of the building.

Historically, smoking food was done for considerable periods of time in order to extend the period during which the food could be eaten. In medieval times, herrings were smoked for several weeks. In order to preserve food as thoroughly as possible, a tradition also developed of using smoking in conjunction with other preserving processes, classically either dry-curing or brine-curing the food before smoking; this can be seen in the European tradition of smoking cured meats, such as bacon or ham. Two ways of smoking developed: hot-smoking, in which the food comes into close contact with both the heat source and the smoke, and cold-smoking, in which the food is exposed to smoke, but not to heat.

Developments in smoking

Advances in the nineteenth century, such as the development of refrigeration and of the railroads, which allowed food to be carried faster from place to place, meant that there was less need to preserve food for as long. Consequently, in the nineteenth century smoking techniques changed, becoming more a way of enhancing the flavor of a food than an essential way of preserving it. The kipper, a cold-smoked herring, is an example of this trend. Another example is smoked salmon, that most luxurious of smoked foods. The technique of cold-smoking salmon evolved independently in many different places. For example, Jewish immigrants from Eastern Europe brought it to Britain in the nineteenth century, at about the same time that people on the West Coast were launching America's own industry using Pacific salmon.

During the twentieth century the mechanical kiln first appeared, powered by electricity and with built-in thermostats. The smoker was thus able to set the internal temperature as required, and this kiln largely, though not entirely, displaced the traditional smokehouses that had been used for centuries.

Modern short cuts

The mechanization and industrialization of smoking foods entailed various short cuts developed to speed up what is, by its nature, a slow, time-consuming process. One such method used to speed up the curing process before smoking is by injecting the food with brine, rather than dry-curing it with salt or immersing it in brine—a practice deplored by artisanal curers. Both curing and smoking are processes that dehydrate food, causing loss of weight. Cynical industrial practice, however, now involves the addition of water-retentive phosphates to brine cure solutions, so that the food stays wetter and thus weighs more; and liquid smoke, made by passing smoke through water, is used to flavor foods easily and speedily, rather than by the process of actually smoking them. The realization that smoking not only preserves food but also deposits a layer of potentially carcinogenic chemicals on the surface of the food being smoked has also resulted in far shorter smoking times than was traditional.

Artisanal smokers

Smoking is a way of changing and enhancing the flavor of the food being smoked; thankfully, there are still artisanal producers committed to producing smoked food using traditional skills and methods, from dry-curing to cold-smoking. The flavor of smoked foods skillfully made with time and care is far superior to those produced using short-cut techniques, making them truly luxuries to be savored and enjoyed.

Right: Pork products such as ham and salami greatly benefit from the processes of smoking and curing

Fuels for smoking

Generally speaking, the smoking of food is done over wood smoke. The reason that wood smoke can preserve food is that the smoke leaves antioxidant and antimicrobial chemical deposits on the surface of the food, which delay the growth of bacterial microbes that would cause the food to decay.

Above: The ideal wood for smoking is hard and free from sap
Opposite: Smoked fish seasoned with pepper

Phenolic compounds in the wood smoke delay the onset of rancidity, which fat is prone to, hence smoking is often used to preserve fat-rich foods, such as cheese, bacon, or oily fish, such as herrings or eels, as well as nonfatty foods, such as game. Since softwoods give an overly resinous flavor to the food being smoked, hardwoods, such as oak, beech, or birch, are best for smoking; in the United States, hickory is the favored wood for smoking. These woods each impart a specific flavor to the food being smoked. It is important to be sure that the wood you are using for smoking food has not been chemically treated, because this would result in unhealthful residues on the food. Aromatics, such as apple wood or herbs, are also used as fuel to enhance the flavor of the food being smoked. The wood for smoking is available in a variety of different forms, including sawdust, briquettes made from compressed sawdust, wood pellets, shavings, chips, and chunks. Other fuel sources for food smoking include peat (a controversial choice in some countries, where peat supplies are depleted), grapevine clippings, and dried seaweed; sometimes all of these are used in addition to wood as aromatics to impart extra flavor.

Hot-smoking

When it comes to smoking food, there are two different types of smoking processes used: hot-smoking and cold-smoking. Hot-smoking is a process in which the food is placed close to the heat source, so that it cooks at the same time as it is being smoked, usually at a temperature of 131–176°F. Since it cooks the food, hot-smoking creates a firm, dry texture in the food being smoked. Hot-smoking can be done at home simply using a covered container, such as a casserole or wok, which is lined with foil, with the "fuel" consisting of rice or aromatics such as tea leaves or spices.

Meet the producer: Black Mountains Smokery

Run by husband-and-wife team Jonathan and Joanna Carthew, this smokery in Wales is noted for the range and quality of its smoked foods.

"The quality of what we start with is important," declares Joanna. "If you start with a rotten product and smoke it, it will still be rotten. We do a lot of commissioned smoking for fishermen, and they often try to give us the less-good fish, but we point out that the really fresh, prime fish will smoke really well. The sourcing is very important to us. We buy farmed fish, not wild, on principle from a reputable fish farm and we don't smoke fish on a Monday because then you're smoking fish that's sat around all weekend. Our ducks come from Gressingham, because we want to support British agriculture; they have a good meat content, not too fat, and a great gamey flavor."

Transforming these raw ingredients into smoked foods involves dry-curing and brining, both using sea salt. "Generally, we dry-cure for cold-smoking and brine for hot-smoking," explains Joanna. "Our house style is a delicate one, which is created both by using a light brine and by not over-smoking. In the old days, smoking was a way of preserving the food, so it was very smoky, very salty in order to keep it safely; we don't need to do that nowadays. Our hot-smoked salmon is mild and our duck breast is very balanced. We don't want to just taste the smoke and the tannins; we want the flavor of the food to come through too.

"We use modern kilns, which work on the same principle as traditional ones, but have the advantage of having a fan so that the smoke is evenly circulated; in the old ones, you had to keep moving the food from the top to the bottom to get an even smoke. We always use oak, which is traditional; we have a good local source of oak. You should always use hardwoods when smoking, not softwoods; otherwise the food would taste like a bubble bath because of all the resin. Our duck breasts are brined for about an hour, cold-smoked for a short time to take away some of the moisture and enhance the smoky flavor, then hot-smoked. You have to keep an eye on everything during the smoking process. We do go home smelling like kippers!"

Cold-smoking

Cold-smoking is a process that takes place below 90°F. During cold-smoking, the food is not heated, just simply exposed to the smoke, with the smoke slowly and gradually affecting the flavor of the food, while the interior texture of the food being smoked is little changed by the smoking process. Probably the best-known example of a cold-smoked food is smoked salmon. Cold-smoking takes longer than hot-smoking, so requires a degree of patience. All smokers agree that cold-smoking is a more complex process than hot-smoking, because of the need to keep a steady source of smoke that is enough to cure the food, but at a temperature that does not exceed 90°F. Furthermore, because constructing a home-made cold smoker to separate the smoke from the direct heat source requires a fair amount of ingenuity, the simplest way for the would-be cold-smoker to practice this craft it is to buy a purpose-built home smoker.

The time taken for both hot- and cold-smoking varies according to the size, weight, and thickness of the food being smoked. The humidity in the atmosphere is another factor that makes for variability in the smoking period, as smoking on a humid day takes longer than on a dry day, due to the fact that the smoke is less dry. It can also be tricky to cold-smoke in very hot weather since the heat in the atmosphere makes the flesh start to cook, creating a seal that prevents the movement of smoke into it and water content out. Both curing and smoking involve a loss of moisture, so a recommended percentage of weight loss at both these stages is often used as a way of assessing whether your food is ready.

Above: The simple combination of smoked salmon and cream cheese is a classic
Right: Fillets of smoked fish

Meet the producer: Richardson's Smokehouse

Based in his grandfather's old smokehouse, in Suffolk, where he works seven days a week, Steve Richardson creates a wide range of smoked foods, from trout to game birds, such as pigeon, using just sea salt and smoke from oak logs, hand-chopped by Steve.

"We've got one smokehouse, divided into two," says Steve, matter of factly. "We do the hot smoking on one side, where we cook the food, and the smoke goes through a vent into the other side, where we cold-smoke it."

Steve works with both sides of his smokehouse to produce results. The kippers are made from herrings —gutted, brined for two hours in a sea-salt solution, then cold-smoked overnight. "Cold-smoking is how you make kippers." The following morning, Steve puts them on trays and they are briefly placed in the hot side of the smokehouse until they take on the level of rich, golden color that Steve wants. "Placing them on the tray means that they keep their oil inside,"

explains Steve. "When you cook my kippers you don't need any butter; they've got enough oil inside." The mackerel at Richardson's is hot-smoked overnight, though again, Steve's intricate knowledge of his smokehouse comes into play. "I shut the fire down, so it's a very low heat, then the next morning I come in and open the fire up." The trick is to increase the temperature gradually, not too quickly, as otherwise the mackerel would "split." Once Steve thinks the mackerel are cooked, he probes them to check they have reached 167°F inside, "That way, I know they're done; it's a 14 to 16 hour process." Different foods are smoked for different periods of time, with his smoked cheeses—a sharp English Cheddar and Long Clawson Stilton—cold-smoked at the shelf at the top of the kiln for six days, while haddock fillets (brined for half an hour) are cold-smoked for 16–18 hours. "We do our smoking the traditional way, the way my grandfather did it," declares Steve. "It takes a long while, I admit, but it's the way fish has always been smoked, and it tastes all the better for it."

Curing with salt

Smoking is traditionally used in conjunction with curing with salt, in the form of either dry-curing or brine-curing. Salt (sodium chloride) is an edible mineral, which has notable preserving properties; and a preliminary curing with salt, either in crystal or brine form, is a key stage of the smoking process. The way that salt works as a preservative is through dehydrating the food with which it comes into contact. Salt operates through osmosis, penetrating the food and drawing out moisture from it, so creating an environment that is inhospitable to the bacteria that cause decay. You may have seen this effect for yourself when sprinkling salt over sliced cucumber or eggplant—a process that draws out the water content from inside these vegetables to the surface.

The choice of salt is an area of individual preference. Salt is either rock salt (salt deposits from within the ground, mined primarily by pumping water into the salt mine to dissolve the salt, then evaporating the resulting brine to create salt crystals) or sea salt, which is obtained by evaporating seawater. The size of the salt crystals in either rock salt or sea salt depends on how the evaporation process took place. If the brine or seawater is rapidly evaporated in a covered container, the salt forms small, fine crystals. If, however, evaporation takes place gradually in an open container, the salt crystallizes to form fragile flakes. The most highly prized sea salts are those that are created due to natural evaporation in shallow, open-air basins through the heat of the sun, a process used particularly in the Mediterranean region. The layer of white crystals at the top of these basins is known as fleur de sel, "flower of salt."

Dry-curing

This process involves coating the food with salt crystals, by both rubbing it in and surrounding the food with salt and then setting it aside. Since salt corrodes metal, it is advisable to ouse ceramic, plastic, or wooden containers, rather than metal ones, for dry-curing. It is customary to weight down the food, pressing it into the salt. At the same time, care has to be taken not to oversalt the food.

The quantity of salt varies according to the thickness of the food being salted. The thin, tail end of a whole fish, for example, needs less salt sprinkled over it than the thicker body part. Depending on how long the dry-curing stage is taking, the liquid extracted by the action of the salt on the food must be removed at regular intervals and fresh, dry salt added as required. The longer the period of dry-curing, the saltier the food will be and the longer its shelf life. Salt cod, for example, is dry-cured in salt for a period of up to 15 days, with the resulting dried fish so intensely salty that it requires extensive soaking to desalinate it before consumption. In the case of smoked foods, the dry-curing stage is usually for a much shorter period, ranging from an hour to a day and night. Flavor is added to the dry-cure stage in the form of sugar, herbs, and aromatics. When cold-smoking fresh wild fish, freezing the fish first for 48 hours in order to kill off any parasites within it is recommended.

Left: Experiment with different varieties of salt and note the effect each one has on flavor
Right: Smoked salmon

Meet the producer: Cley Smokehouse

Fish and seafood are the stars of the show at this Norfolk coastal smokery, owned and run by Glen Weston, fisherman turned smoker.

"We always use prime fish," says Glen. "We're predominantly a shellfish coast here, so we take full advantage of that. Our smoked prawns [shrimp] are one of our best-selling lines." Glen's smoking equipment consists of two traditional cold-smoking chimneys and a separate mini kiln, used for both hot- and cold-smoking, always over oak.

"We don't brine for very long and we don't smoke for very long," explains Glen, "so all our smoked fish has a very subtle flavor. I use a weak brine—about 65 percent salt content—for all my wet-brining. It's important to brine, as it gives the fish a glaze." Cley Smokehouse is particularly noted for its traditional smoked fish, such as buckling (hot-smoked herrings with their heads removed and their roes inside) and kippers. "The kippers are brined for 15 minutes, placed on tenters (racks) straightaway, dried for half an hour, then cold-smoked for 5–6 hours overnight. I come in in the morning and judge whether they're ready or not. To get the desired effect when cold-smoking, you want to smoke for as slowly as possible for as long as possible. We could smoke kippers in three hours, but they'd dry out and get a harsh flavor. When you cold-smoke haddock, it really dries out if you overdo it; of all the fish we do, it needs to be smoked really gently.

"There's no thermostat in my chimneys," quips Glen. "I go by touch and sight. Cold-smoking is not an exact science; it's a very subtle process. The weather affects the smoking process. In summer, when it's hotter, it takes longer to cold-smoke, so we leave the fish in the brine a little longer than in the winter, to increase the keeping properties of the salt. Every smokehouse has its own style, its own way of doing things, and their smoked foods taste different from each other. What gives me the most satisfaction— makes all the hard work worthwhile—is when someone comes into the shop and says, 'Your kipper was the best kipper I've ever tasted.' "

Brine-curing

Brine-curing involves immersing the food to be cured in brine, which is a solution of salt in water. It is important that the brine solution be strong enough, that is salty enough, to preserve effectively. Recommended ratios of salt to water for an effective brine are 7–9 oz. (about ⅝–¾ cup) of salt for every quart of water. The salt must be thoroughly dissolved in the water, and to speed up this process it is possible to use warm or hot water, though it is very important than the brine be cooled down thoroughly before the food is immersed in it. Again, as with dry-salting, it is important to avoid metal containers because of the risk of salt corrosion; and the brining should take place in a refrigerator or other cool place.

The brining period depends on the length and thickness of what is being brined and the flavoring wanted. When brining, the food should be submerged totally and the brine should also be stirred regularly during the brining period to distribute the salt evenly. Because brine-curing is a quicker way of curing than dry-curing, penetrating the meat faster, it is traditionally used for larger cuts of meat, such as whole joints. Flavor is added to brine cures by using alcohol, such as hard cider, wine, or beer, as part of the liquid content of the brine mixture. Spices, herbs, and flavorings such as sugar, a popular addition, can also be added to the brine cure.

This preliminary stage of either dry-curing or brine-curing is an important part of the smoking process, preserving the food, adding flavor, and also preparing it for smoking. Having been cured, the food is rinsed, patted dry, and often set aside to dry off, ideally in well-ventilated conditions – a process that allows the protein drawn to the surface by salting to form a natural glaze known as a pellicule. This pellicule forms a protective surface over the food, containing its fat and also acting as a surface to which the smoke can adhere. Once dried, the cured food is then either hot-smoked or cold-smoked, as described above.

Right: A basic setup for smoking salmon in the home

Home smoking

The smoking process offers the would-be home smoker many opportunities for experimentation. To start with, of course, there is the choice of foodstuffs to be smoked, though do bear in mind that for succulent results, it is advisable to choose a naturally fatty or oil-rich food.

Dry-curing or brine-curing is the next area of choice, with both being an important way of adding flavor to the food being smoked and preparing it for the smoking process. Foods that have been already cooked, such as cooked shrimp, do not need curing in this way and can simply be smoked. Having cured your food, you can then choose whether to cold-smoke or to hot-smoke. Note that professional smokers warn against the risks of both overcuring and oversmoking.

Sourcing the ingredients

For the best results, experienced smokers recommend using fresh, good-quality ingredients, such as prime fish (post-rigor mortis) or poultry, for the smoking process, rather than using second-rate ingredients and hoping that the smoking process will mask their shortcomings.

Above: Sea salt and pepper
Opposite: Gravlax—cured salmon, which is popular in Nordic countries

While good ingredients are a basic starting point, it is advisable first to build up your expertise in smoking using affordable ingredients, such as mackerel or trout, before experimenting on costly ingredients, such as wild salmon or game. In choosing which salt to use for curing, purity is an important factor to bear in mind. The process by which sea salt is produced and refined commercially ensures the removal of the bitter minerals otherwise found in sea salt. Coarse sea salt crystals are often used in dry-curing. Unrefined sea salt, characteristically gray in color, is coated in minerals such as magnesium chloride and sulfate and has a more complex flavor than refined salt. The fine table salt used as an everyday condiment usually contains anti-caking agents, most of which do not dissolve as quickly as salt, so can cause a cloudy brine.

How to store

Although curing and smoking have their preserving qualities, it is important to refrigerate your own-smoked food and eat it within a few days of smoking. If you plan to keep smoked food for longer than a few days, you should freeze it. One of the joys of smoking foods yourself is that freshly smoked food has a wonderful flavor, best enjoyed fresh from the smoker.

Special equipment

The Internet is the simplest and best way to track down specialized smoking equipment, such as an electric home smoker or smoking bags (sealable, wood-filled bags designed for use in the home oven).

Making hot-smoked salmon

Hot-smoking salmon gives it a wonderful rich color and a great smoky flavor. You can serve the salmon either hot or cold. To hot-smoke, you can use a vegetable steamer or a roasting tray with a wire rack and aluminum foil. Using an old vegetable steamer is good because it can be used on top of the stove, the top pan (the steam part with the holes) will be big enough to capture all the smoke, and you can check it's all OK just by lifting the lid. While this technique is quite easy to do at home or in the backyard, do be aware that, as the name suggests, hot-smoking does become quite smoky. If you have a sensitive smoke alarm, rig up a burner in the backyard instead, or even use your barbecue as an impromptu outdoor smoker.

2 fresh salmon steaks

salt and pepper

2 handfuls of wood chips,
such as oak or alder

lemon rind

fresh thyme

Equipment needed

old vegetable steamer or a roasting
tray with a rack and aluminum foil

Serves 2

1 Season the salmon steaks with salt and pepper and place back in the refrigerator while you prepare your smoker.

2 Place the wood chips in the bottom of the steamer pan or roasting tray with the lemon rind and thyme, and place on high heat until they are hot and smoking (this takes about 10 minutes).

3 Place the salmon in the top part of the steamer or on the wire rack, if using, cover with the lid or foil, and leave over the heat for six minutes.

4 Turn off the heat, but leave the lid or foil on and the salmon still over the wood chips for another 20 minutes, so that the smoke can infuse the salmon. The salmon can be served hot or cold.

Making cold-smoked bacon

Cold-smoking is more difficult than hot and needs a more complex gadget or a purpose-built smoke box with a thermostat. Consider using a barbecue with a hose about 10 feet long, a large metal drum, aluminum foil and a temperature probe, just to make sure you can control the temperature. The key to cold-smoking is keeping the heat away from the food. You don't want to cook it, just to funnel the smoke so you can impart the flavor. Ideally, you want the temperature in the smoke chamber to be at about 68–77°F.

2 lb. home-cured bacon
(see page 176)

Equipment needed
your smoking box or
homemade gadget

Serves 4

1 First, you need to get the wood chips smoking. If you're doing it on a barbecue, use charcoal as your heat source. As the coals turn white, place wood chips on aluminum foil on the cooking rack above them to make the smoke. It's best to soak the wood chips so they smoke for longer; and it's a good idea to keep a water spray nearby to damp them down should the temperature rise too high.

2 Then attach a hose from the barbecue vent. Place your cured bacon in the metal drum on a rack covered with foil. Make a hole in the foil and add the hose to the drum, making sure that the drum is completely sealed so the smoke remains inside. Add a temperature probe, if you have one, so you can control the heat. Smoking is down to personal taste, as well as the wood and size of meat, but two hours is a rough guide. Store the bacon in an airtight container in the refrigerator; it should last up to a week.

Making home-cured bacon

Curing your own Canadian bacon is both straightforward and satisfying. The cured bacon can then be cooked as it is or smoked to taste, if desired.

⅛ scant cup rock salt

⅛ cup curing salt

1 scant tablespoon brown crystal sugar

2 lb. pork loin

Equipment needed

non-corrosive container

muslin

Makes 2 lb.

1 Assemble the salts and sugar to make the cure.

2 Combine the cure ingredients, then rub the cure into both sides of the pork. If you have the rind still on or thick parts of the loin, pierce the rind with a skewer to ensure that the cure penetrates into the meat.

3 Place the pork in a non-corrosive container for 1 week and leave, covered with plastic wrap, in the bottom of the fridge. When the time is up, wipe the loin clean and dry it thoroughly with paper towels or muslin. Wrap it in muslin to protect it, and hang for 2–3 weeks (the longer, the better) in a cold place or in the fridge. After hanging, the bacon is ready to cook, or you can then smoke it (see page 174).

Making brine-cured pork side

The simple step of brine-curing the pork before roasting it makes it both very tender and flavorful.

½ cup curing salt

4 cups water

2 lb. fresh side pork, off the bone

4 cloves

1 teaspoon chopped fennel leaves

8 sage leaves

1 teaspoon chopped fresh
rosemary leaves

3 garlic cloves

1 tablespoon olive oil

Equipment needed

plastic or ceramic container

pestle and mortar

Serves 4

1 First, make the brine by bringing the curing salt to the boil in the water. Once boiled, leave it to cool. When it has cooled, transfer the liquid to a plastic or ceramic container and add the pork, making sure it is completely covered with the liquid. The pork can be left for 1–7 days at the bottom of the refrigerator, depending on the time you have. You will get better results the longer you leave it. When it comes out of the brine, you will need to soak it again overnight in fresh water. Once it has been soaked again, prepare it for roasting by drying it thoroughly with muslin or paper towels, then leaving it to air dry in the kitchen for an hour.

2 Preheat the oven to 350°F. Mix the rest of the ingredients using a pestle and mortar.

3 Rub the mixture over the pork, then roast for 2 hours. Allow 30 minutes to rest before serving.

Using your produce

Tartare of salmon with cucumber salad

This recipe, adapted from Raymond Blanc's magical *Recipes from Le Manoir aux Quat'Saisons*, involves dry-curing (see page 167). He stipulates wild salmon, but I think that, because it is marinated, this is slightly extravagant. Fillet of salmon is essential for this recipe, and since it is easier to make if you have a matching pair to lay one on top of the other, I suggest buying a whole tail and asking the fishmonger to fillet and skin it for you.

1 lb. farmed salmon tail piece, filleted and skinned

1½ tablespoons chopped fresh dill

zest and juice of 1 lemon

1 tablespoon superfine sugar

coarse sea salt and freshly ground white pepper

½ teaspoon Dijon mustard

3 tablespoons sour cream

For the cucumber salad

½ large (or 1 small) cucumber

coarse sea salt and freshly ground white pepper

1 teaspoon white wine vinegar

2 tablespoons safflower oil

8 sprigs of dill

Equipment needed

tweezers

Serves 8

1 Remove any stray pin bones from the salmon with a pair of tweezers, then lay the fillets flat on a plate. Mix 1 tablespoon of the dill together with the lemon zest, sugar, and about 1 tablespoon of salt, and rub the mixture over both sides of the salmon. Place one fillet on top of the other, cover with foil, and leave to marinate in the refrigerator for 12 hours.

2 At the end of this time, unwrap the salmon and rinse it under cold running water to remove the salt. Drain it well, pat dry with paper towels, and cut it into thin strips, about 1 in. long.

3 In a large bowl, mix the lemon juice with the mustard, 2 teaspoons of the sour cream, the remaining dill, and a little pepper, and stir in the salmon. Leave in a cool place for 1 hour.

4 Meanwhile, prepare the cucumber by cutting it in half lengthwise and scooping out the seeds with a teaspoon. Slice it finely, put in a colander, sprinkle over about 1 teaspoon of salt, and let it stand for 30 minutes. Then rinse under cold running water, drain, and pat dry. Put the cucumber slices in a small bowl, add the vinegar, oil, and a little pepper and mix thoroughly.

5 Raymond Blanc serves the salmon stunningly presented in individual molds: very effective but surprisingly simple. Using a 2-in. pastry cutter as a mold, place it in the center of a plate and fill it almost up to the top with the salmon, pressing down gently with the back of a teaspoon to pack the fish firmly. Spread 1 teaspoon of sour cream on the top, smoothing it with a spatula, then carefully lift off the pastry cutter. Arrange slices of cucumber around the base and decorate the top with a sprig of dill. Serve with slices of toasted brioche.

Classic gravlax

Gravlax is a classic Swedish dish of raw marinated salmon flavored with dill, prepared using a dry cure (see page 167). In pre-refrigerator days, the salmon package would be buried in the cold ground to mature. These days, it is fashionable to cure gravlax for a shorter time, but it gains more flavor and a firmer texture if left for 48 hours.

2 fillets of fresh salmon, 1 lb. each, skin on

¼ scant cup sugar

¼ rounded cup coarse sea salt

2 tablespoons black peppercorns, crushed

1 large bunch of fresh dill

For the gravlaxsas (gravlax sauce)

¼ rounded cup Dijon mustard

1 teaspoon dried English mustard

3 tablespoons superfine sugar

2 tablespoons white wine vinegar

3 tablespoons sunflower oil

3 tablespoons light olive oil

3 tablespoons chopped fresh dill

Equipment needed:

tweezers

Serves 12

1 Using tweezers, remove any remaining bones from the salmon, then put one fillet, skin side down, on a large, double sheet of plastic wrap. Mix the sugar, salt, and crushed peppercorns in a bowl, then spread evenly over the flesh. Sprinkle the dill over the top. Arrange the other fillet on top to form a sandwich and wrap up tightly in the plastic wrap. Transfer to a non-metal dish and put a small tray and a weight, such as a medium-size can of food, on top. Refrigerate for 48 hours, turning over every 12 hours. The salmon will then be ready to eat, but the longer it sits in the marinade, the stronger the flavor will be.

2 To make the gravlaxsas, mix the mustards, sugar, and vinegar in a bowl. Slowly beat in the oils as if making mayonnaise, until the sauce is thick. Stir in the dill and refrigerate until needed (you may need to beat it again before serving).

3 Unwrap the fish, reserving the juices, and scrape off the excess peppercorns and herbs. Slice the salmon vertically toward the skin, about ¼ in. thick, then slice close to the skin horizontally to release the slice. Serve on rye bread with slices of pickled cucumber and the gravlaxsas.

4 Gravlax keeps well, wrapped, in the refrigerator for at least 3 days. Slice the salmon as you need it, keeping it with the juices and tightly wrapping after each use. Foil tends to pit with the corrosive salt, so use plastic wrap.

Variation:

Horseradish and juniper pickled salmon

Finely grate the rind of 2 lemons and put in a bowl with 20 crushed juniper berries, 2 tablespoons sugar, ¼ rounded cup coarse sea salt, 2 tablespoons white peppercorns, crushed, and about ½ cup gin. Wrap and chill as in the main recipe. To serve, mix 2 tablespoons horseradish sauce or creamed horseradish with the grated rind of 1 lemon. Slice the fish as in the previous recipe and serve on thinly sliced rye bread or pumpernickel with the sauce.

Kedgeree

Despite its Hindi name, kedgeree is evidently a Scottish invention, taken to India by Scottish soldiers in colonial times. Traditionally finnan haddie (smoked haddock) is the fish used, but you can substitute another smoked fish.

½ lb. finnan haddie (or other smoked fish)

1 small onion, sliced

3 black peppercorns

bay leaf

1¼ cups milk

1 cup rice

1 stick butter, melted

3 tablespoons heavy cream

3 hard-boiled eggs, chopped

3 tablespoons minced curly parsley

salt and freshly ground black pepper

cayenne pepper

Serves 6

1 Put the fish in a saucepan along with the onion, peppercorns, bay leaf, and milk. Place over medium heat and bring almost to the boil. Turn down the heat and simmer gently for about 5–7 minutes, until the fish is cooked. Drain the fish, discarding the onion, bay leaf, and peppercorns. Reserve the milk and leave the fish to cool. Meanwhile, boil the rice in salted water and drain thoroughly.

2 When the fish is cool enough to handle, remove the skin and any bones and flake it gently into sizable chunks by hand; do not be too rough or break the fish down into too small pieces or it will disintegrate when you stir it into the rice.

3 In a clean pan, melt the butter over medium heat, add the cream, a couple of tablespoons of the reserved milk, and the rice and stir until it is thoroughly coated with the mixture. Carefully fold in the flaked fish, the hard-boiled eggs, and the parsley, and cook over low heat for 1 minute. Adjust the seasoning and serve sprinkled with cayenne pepper.

Salted duck

Recipes for salt duck date back to the nineteenth century. The Chinese have a similar recipe, using a mixture of salt and 5-spice powder, but one favorite version comes from Denmark, where they salt the duck and marinate it in honey. The result of this dry-curing (see also page 167) is a pungent duck, soft as butter, which literally falls away from its carcass.

1 plump fresh duck, weighing approximately 4½ lb.

¼ rounded cup rock salt

For the marinade

4 tablespoons honey

7 cups water

5 bay leaves

8 juniper berries, crushed

1 onion, stuck with cloves

1 carrot, finely sliced

1 cup wine vinegar

Serves 4

1 Wipe the duck with a paper towel; then, using a sharp knife, make deep incisions all over its skin. Rub the rock salt all over the duck, both inside and out, cramming it into the incisions.

2 Meanwhile, melt the honey in the water in a casserole dish, and, when it is dissolved, add the bay leaves, juniper berries, onion, and carrot. Simmer the marinade for about 5 minutes, then remove it from the heat and add the wine vinegar. Leave to cool before submerging the duck in the liquid. Leave the duck to marinate for about 3–4 days in a cool place, making sure that it is completely covered in liquid.

3 Drain the duck, carefully skin it, and remove the outer loose fat. This should be done just before cooking; otherwise the flesh will harden. Either return the duck to the marinade (which gives it a sharper, saltier flavor) or place it in a casserole filled with fresh water. Bring to the boil and cook over a low heat or bake it in a slow oven at 300°F for about 2 hours. Serve either hot or cold with rice.

Mackerel and bulgur wheat salad

The creamy horseradish dressing in this recipe is a fabulous complement to the richness of the smoked mackerel, while the raw vegetables add crunch and color. If you wish, you can use couscous instead of bulgur wheat.

⅜ cup bulgur wheat

1 tablespoon freshly squeezed lemon juice

1 tablespoon minced fresh chives

¼ yellow bell pepper, deseeded and diced

8 radishes, sliced

½ cup spinach leaves

¾ lb. smoked mackerel fillets, flaked

For the dressing

3 tablespoons low-fat cream cheese

2 teaspoons horseradish sauce

1 teaspoon minced fresh chives

freshly ground black pepper, to serve

Serves 2

1 Cook the bulgur wheat in a saucepan of lightly salted boiling water for 15 minutes or until tender. Drain, then mix with the lemon juice, chives, bell pepper, and radishes.

2 Put the spinach leaves into shallow salad bowls, spoon the bulgur wheat on top, then add the flaked smoked mackerel. Mix the dressing ingredients together and drizzle over the fish. Finish with a grinding of black pepper.

Jasmine-brined roasted poussins with salsa verde

Poussin is the French word for a very young chicken. Brine-curing (see page 169) the poussins ensures a crisp skin when roasted. You can use any tea to make the brine, but jasmine tea infuses a floral taste into the poussins and creates a subtle flavor when cooked. Serve with the dark green salsa verde. You can also make this with Cornish game hen.

2 small broiler chickens, weighing 1½ lb. each
(or 1 Cornish game hen)
1 small unwaxed lemon
1 garlic clove, crushed
1 tablespoon olive oil
coarse sea salt and freshly ground black pepper

For the brining solution
4 tablespoons jasmine tea or 4 jasmine tea bags
6 cups boiling water
¼ scant cup coarse rock salt
1 tablespoon dark brown sugar

For the salsa verde
1 large handful fresh flat-leaf parsley leaves
1 large handful cilantro leaves
1 large handful fresh mint leaves
2 garlic cloves, minced
1 tablespoon brined capers
½ cup olive oil

Equipment needed
food processor
kitchen string

Serves 2

1 First make the brine. Put the jasmine tea in a large measuring pitcher and pour the boiling water over. Add the rock salt and sugar and stir until dissolved. Set aside to cool completely.

2 Wash and dry the chickens and put in a deep dish. Pour the cooled brine over them, cover, and refrigerate for 6–8 hours.

3 When you are ready to cook, preheat the oven to 375°F.

4 Remove the chickens from the brining mixture and pat dry, removing any leftover tea leaves. Discard the brining mixture; it cannot be used again.

5 Place the chickens in a roasting pan. Peel off the zest of the lemon and reserve for the salsa verde. Cut the lemon into quarters and stuff the cavities with them. Tie the legs together with kitchen string. Mix together the garlic and oil and rub over the skin of the chickens. Season with salt and pepper.

6 Roast in the preheated oven for 35 minutes until the chickens are cooked and the juices run clear.

7 To make the salsa verde, put all the salsa ingredients in a food processor and pulse until roughly chopped. Be careful not to overprocess; you want the salsa to be slightly chunky. Season with salt and pepper.

8 When the chickens are ready, remove them from the oven and set aside in a warm place to rest for 10 minutes, covered with aluminum foil. Carve and serve with the salsa verde.

Traditional fish pie

For comfort food the traditional British fish "pie" (no crust is involved) takes some beating. This version, which includes hard-boiled eggs and a hint of mustard, is just the thing to warm a wintry evening.

2 cups milk

1 lb. 10 oz. finnan haddie (or other smoked fish), skinned

2 sticks plus 2 tablespoons unsalted butter

1 tablespoon English mustard powder

4 tablespoons all-purpose flour

2 hard-boiled eggs, peeled and quartered

2 lb. high-starch (floury) potatoes

coarse sea salt and freshly ground black pepper

Serves 4

1 Preheat the oven to 400°F.

2 Put the milk in a wide saucepan, heat just to boiling point, then add the fish. Turn off the heat and leave the fish to poach until opaque—do not overcook.

3 Meanwhile, melt 1 stick of the butter in another saucepan, then stir in the mustard and flour. Remove from the heat and strain the poaching liquid into the pan.

4 Arrange the fish and eggs in a shallow baking dish or casserole.

5 Return the pan to the heat. Whisking vigorously to smooth out any lumps, bring the mixture to the boil. Season to taste, but take care because it may be salty enough. Pour the sauce into the casserole and mix carefully with the fish and eggs.

6 Cook the potatoes in boiling salted water until soft, then drain. Return to the pan. Melt the remaining butter in a small pan. Reserve 4 tablespoons of this butter and stir the remainder into the potatoes. Mash well and season. Spoon the mixture carefully over the sauced fish, brush with the reserved butter, and transfer to the oven. Cook for 20 minutes, or until nicely browned.

Note: If you can't find finnan haddie, you can sprinkle ¼ lb. smoked salmon, finely sliced, over poached fresh haddock just before adding the sauce.

Useful addresses

United States

There are over 6,000 farmers' markets in the U.S., with new ones opening up every week. Check the following websites to find your nearest one.

California Farmers' Markets
www.cafarmersmarkets.com

Chef2Chef Farmers' Market Directory
www.chef2chef.net/marketplace/farmer-markets

Local Harvest Farmers' Market Directory
www.localharvest.org

United States Agricultural Marketing Service
www.ams.usda.gov/farmersmarkets

It would be an impossible task to list all the famers' markets in the U.S., but here is a list of ones that come highly recommended:

Alemany Farmers' Market
100 Alemany Blvd
San Francisco CA 94110
www.sfgsa.org/index.aspx?page=1058

Barton Creek Farmers' Market
2901 S Capital of Texas Hwy
Austin, TX 78746
www.bartoncreekfarmersmarket.org

Boulder County Farmers' Market
13th St between Arapahoe and Canyon
Boulder, CO 80302
www.boulderfarmers.org

Capital City Farmers' Market
60 State St
Montpelier, VT 05602
www.montpelierfarmersmarket.com

Carrboro Farmers' Market
301 W Main St
Carrboro, NC 27510
www.carrborofarmersmarket.com

Chattanooga Market
First Tennessee Pavilion
1829 Carter St
Chattanooga, TN 37408
www.chattanoogamarket.com

Crescent City Farmers' Market
700 Magazine St
New Orleans, LA 70130
www.crescentcityfarmersmarket.org

Dane County Farmers' Market
Capitol Square
Madison WI 53701
www.dcfm.org

Dupont Circle Freshfarm Market
1560 20th St NW
Washington, DC 20036
www.freshfarmmarkets.org

Fernandina Farmers' Market
Corner of Centre and 7th St
Fernandina Beach, FL 32034
www.fernandinafarmersmarket.com

Flint Farmers' Market
420 E Boulevard Drive
Flint, MI 48507
www.flintfarmersmarket.com

Forsyth Farmers' Market
South End of Forsyth Park
Savannah, GA
www.forsythfarmersmarket.org

Green City Market
1790 N Clark St
Lincoln Park
Chicago, IL 60614
www.chicagogreencitymarket.org

Pee Dee State Farmers' Market
2513 W Lucas St (US Hwy 52)
Florence, SC 29501
www.pdfarmersmarket.sc.gov

Portland Farmers' Market
SW Park Ave and SW Montgomery St
Portland, OR 97201
www.portlandfarmersmarket.org

Reading Terminal Market
51 N 12th St
Philadelphia, PA 19107
www.readingterminalmarket.org

Saint Paul Farmers' Market
290 E 5th St
Saint Paul, MN 55101
www.stpaulfarmersmarket.com

San Luis Obispo Farmers' Market
Higuera St
San Luis Opispo CA
www.slocountyfarmers.org

Santa Cruz River Farmers' Market
1352 W Speedway Blvd
Tucson, AZ 85745
www.communityfoodbank.com

Santa Monica Farmers' Markets
Various locations
Contact the administrative office on
310 458 8712 or check the website
below for details
www01.smgov.net/farmers_market

Soulard Farmers' Market
730 Carroll St
St Louis, MO 63104
www.soulardmarket.com

Union Square Greenmarket
E 17th St and Broadway
New York, NY 10003
www.grownyc.org/greenmarket

Santa Fe Farmers' Market
1607 Paseo de Peralta
Santa Fe, NM 87501
www.santafefarmersmarket.com

University District Farmers' Market
Corner of University Way and 50th St
Seattle, WA 98105
www.seattlefarmersmarkets.org/
markets/u_district

Canada

Farmers' Markets Canada
Useful resource for finding your
nearest market
www.farmersmarketscanada.ca

Calgary Farmers' Market
H6, 4421 Quesnay Wood Drive SW
Calgary, AB
T3E 7K4
www.calgaryfarmersmarket.ca

Halifax Farmers' Market
1209 Marginal Road/Pier 20
Halifax, NS
B3L 4T6
www.halifaxfarmersmarket.com

Le Marché du Vieux Port
160 Quai St-André
Quebec City, QC
G1K 3Y2
www.marchevieuxport.com

Marché St Norbert Farmers'
Market
3514 Pembina Hwy
Winnipeg
R3V 1L5
www.stnorbertfarmersmarket.ca

Saskatoon Farmers' Market
414 Ave B South
Saskatoon, SK
S7M 1M8
www.saskatoonfarmersmarket.com

Saint John City Market
47 Charlotte Street
Saint John, NB
E2L 2H8
www.sjcitymarket.com

St Lawrence Market
92 Front Street East
Toronto ON
M5E 1C4
www.stlawrencemarket.com

Vancouver Farmers Markets
Various locations
www.eatlocal.org

Other useful websites

British Corner Shop
www.britishcornershop.com
For imported British food products,
such as Granary Flour

Canning Pantry
www.canningpantry.com
Suppliers of mason jars and other
canning materials

The Cook's Thesaurus
www.foodsubs.com
Illustrated listings of food items with
suggested substitutions

FoodLovers Britain
PO Box 66303
London NW6 9PD
www.FoodLoversBritain.com

Le Parfait
http://leparfait.com
Leading manufacturer of French-
style canning jars; site offers
step-by-step canning techniques

Mackenzie Limited
www.mackenzieltd.com
Importers of foreign delicacies, such
as finnan haddie and fine cheeses

National Center for Home Food
Preservation
www.uga.edu/nchfp
Authoritative information on
canning procedures and food safety

OChef
www.ochef.com
Interactive site offering "Answers to
Life's Vexing Cooking Questions"

Practically Edible
www.practicallyedible.com
Great encyclopedia of food facts

Index

Acknowledgments

Henrietta Green:
Thanks to all the craft producers who shared their secrets, and to the staff at Cico: Cindy Richards, Gillian Haslam, and Pete Jorgensen.

Jenny Linford:
My heartfelt thanks to all the food producers I talked to for their time and patience: Cothi Valley Goats, Ivy House Dairy Farm, Neal's Yard Creamery, Staff of Life, Richard Bertinet, Long Crichel, The Toffee Shop, Sweet Treats, Paul A. Young, Wendy Brandon, Seafares, England Preserves, Lidgate's, Trealy Farm, Baxter's Potted Shrimps, Black Mountains Smokery, Richardson's Smokehouse, and Cley Smokehouse.

Picture credits

Key: a=above, b=below, r=right, l=left, c=center

Martin Brigdale 42, 53bl, 54, 55al, 55ar, 60al, 60ar, 60bc, 60br, 61al, 61ar, 134, 153
Peter Cassidy 65, 66, 71l, 75, 76, 95, 101l, 102, 105, 135, 137, 138, 139, 140, 141, 154, 161, 168, 170
Gus Filgate 63
Tara Fisher 18
Jonathan Gregson 164, 171
Winfried Heinze 72, 73, 74l, 91, 96
Richard Jung 40, 48, 100, 157
Gavin Kingcome 7r, 10, 12r, 13, 14, 15, 16, 17, 19, 20, 27br, 36, 37, 38, 41, 43, 44, 45, 46, 47, 49, 51, 70, 78, 81, 104, 132, 133, 142, 143, 158, 163, 165, 167
William Lingwood 34, 181, 185
David Munns 121

Noel Murphy 21
Gloria Nicol 92, 101r, 103, 106, 107, 108, 109, 110, 111, 125, 126, 127, 129
William Reavell 183
Claire Richardson 166
Lucinda Symons 114
Debi Treloar 31
Ian Wallace 162
Stuart West 1, 2, 4, 5, 6, 7l, 8, 9, 22, 23, 24, 25, 26, 27al, 27ar, 27bl, 28, 29, 50, 52al, 52r, 55b, 56, 57, 58, 59, 60bl, 61r, 68, 74r, 82, 83, 84, 85, 87, 88, 89, 90, 98, 112, 113, 115, 116, 117, 118, 119, 120, 121, 122, 123, 130, 144, 145, 146, 147, 148, 149, 150, 151, 169, 172, 173, 174, 175, 176, 177, 178, 179
Kate Whitaker 33, 97
Polly Wreford 71r

Recipe credits

Key: r=right, l=left

Valerie Aikman-Smith 93r, 184
Maxine Clarke 63, 95, 153, 181
Linda Collister 54, 56, 94
Ross Dobson 157
Liz Franklin 34
Henrietta Green 30, 32, 35, 52, 62, 64, 67, 116, 124r, 126, 128r, 146, 152, 155, 156, 180, 182
Rachael Anne Hill 183

Jenny Linford 22, 24, 26, 28, 58, 60, 82, 151
Hannah Miles 97
Gloria Nicol 92, 120, 122, 124l, 125, 127, 128l, 129
Louise Pickford 93l
Fiona Smith 154
Sonia Stevenson 185
Nicki Trench 84, 91, 96
Louise Wagstaffe 86, 89, 112, 118, 144, 149, 172, 174, 177, 178
Fran Warde 31
Laura Washburn 65, 66

Additional credits

Home economist: Louise Wagstaffe 22–29, 52–61 82–90, 112–123, 144–151, 172–179
Stylist: Luis Peral-Aranda 22–29, 52–61 82–90, 112–123, 144–151, 172–179